Praise for *Yes!*

"I recommend the book highly, as it presents all kinds of clever and effective influence tactics. You can learn everything from the virtues of inconveniencing people to why restaurants shouldn't offer a basket of mints for people on the way out, to how to use—and how not to use—fear as a motivator. *Yes!* is based on the best behavioral science research and is an easy read."

—Robert Sutton, author of *The No Asshole Rule*

"*Yes!* is the single best introduction to and distillation of research and wisdom on how to change people's minds, including your own."

—Warren Bennis, Distinguished Professor of Business, University of Southern California, author of *On Becoming a Leader* and coauthor of *Judgment: How Winning Leaders Make Great Calls*

"I've recommended many books but this one is among the best I've found . . . try to read it before everyone else does. It's chock full of useful advice tested by leading researchers."

—*Working Class*

"If you had a team of bright guys looking for research that you can actually use to improve your effectiveness, and they wrote it up for you with wit and style, putting in nifty little reports of three to five pages, would that be useful? YES! This book is the trifecta: first-rate research, lively writing, and practical advice. Read it, enjoy it, use it."

—Dale Dauten, nationally syndicated King Features columnist and author of *The Gifted Boss*

Yes!

50 Scientifically Proven Ways to Be Persuasive

Noah J. Goldstein, PhD,

Steve J. Martin, and

Robert B. Cialdini, PhD

Free Press

New York London Toronto Sydney

FREE PRESS

A Division of Simon & Schuster, Inc.
1230 Avenue of the Americas
New York, NY 10020

First Free Press trade paperback edition January 2010

FREE PRESS and colophon are
trademarks of Simon & Schuster, Inc.

For information about special discounts for bulk purchases,
please contact Simon & Schuster Special Sales at
1-866-506-1949 or business@simonandschuster.com.

The Simon & Schuster Speakers Bureau can bring authors
to your live event. For more information or to book an event
contact the Simon & Schuster Speakers Bureau at
1-866-248-3049 or visit our website at www.simonspeakers.com.

Book design by Ellen R. Sasahara

Manufactured in the United States of America

17   19   20   18

The Library of Congress has catalogued the hardcover edition as follows:
Goldstein, Noah J.
Yes!: 50 scientifically proven ways to be persuasive /
Noah J. Goldstein,
Steve J. Martin, and Robert B. Cialdini.
p. cm.
Includes bibliographical references and index.
1. Business communication. 2. Persuasion (Psychology).
3. Marketing. 4. Interpersonal communication. I. Martin, Steve J.
II. Cialdini, Robert B. III. Title.
HF5718.G65 2008
658. 4'5—dc22   2007041917

ISBN 978-1-4165-7096-7
ISBN 978-1-4165-7614-3 (pbk)
ISBN 978-1-4165-7112-4 (ebook)

For my parents and, of course, for Jenessa – NJG

For my niece and nephew Casie Leigh and Riley – SJM

For my granddaughter Hailey Brooke Cialdini – RBC

Contents

Contents

Contents

Contents

Preface

According to John Lennon, the moment he first began falling in love with Yoko Ono occurred at an installation of her work at a London art gallery in 1966. One piece in the exhibition required viewers to climb to the top of a dimly lit, shaky ladder and then to peer through a spyglass into a small area of the ceiling, where a single word was displayed in barely perceptible letters.

The word was small and simple. But it struck Lennon with so much force that, although he didn't fall physically from the ladder, he began to fall emotionally for the woman who had arranged for him to see that word under those conditions—because he immediately resonated with her recognition of its healing power in a darkly dangerous, ominously unstable world.

That word was not "love," as most people think. Instead, it was a word that both leads to and flows from love and, fortunately, is much more obtainable.

The word was "yes."

Just because yes is simple and obtainable, we shouldn't be fooled into believing that anyone can easily secure it from others—at least not without knowing certain secrets of the persuasion process. The primary purpose of this book is to give readers access to fifty secrets to successful persuasion that have been validated in scientific studies and that can be used in wholly ethical ways. Even though, as the book's authors, we wouldn't try to turn John Lennon's famous lyric into the claim "All you need is *Yes!*," we are confident that readers who understand and properly employ the book's lessons will become markedly more persuasive at work, at home, and elsewhere.

Introduction

There's an old joke told by the nightclub comic Henny Youngman, who referred to his accommodations from the previous night by saying, "What a hotel! The towels were so big and fluffy I could hardly close my suitcase."

Over the last few years, the moral dilemma facing hotel guests has changed. These days, the question of whether to *remove* the towels from their room has been replaced by the question of whether to *reuse* the towels during the course of their stay. With the increasing adoption of environmental programs by hotels, more and more travelers are being asked to reuse their towels to help conserve environmental resources, save energy, and reduce the amount of detergent-related pollutants released into the environment. In most cases, this request comes in the form of cards placed in guests' bathrooms—cards that provide some surprising insights into the remarkable science of persuasion.

A survey of the persuasive messages conveyed by dozens of request cards from a wide variety of hotels around the globe reveals that these cards most commonly attempt to encourage towel recycling efforts by focusing guests almost exclusively on the importance of environmental protection. In other words, guests are almost invariably informed that reusing their towels will conserve natural resources and help spare the environment from further depletion, disruption, and corruption. To further draw guests' attention to the impact of towel recycling on the environment, this information is often accompanied by various eye-catching, environment-related pictures in the background, ranging from rainbows to raindrops to rainforests . . . to reindeer.

This persuasion strategy generally seems to be an effective one. For example, one of the largest manufacturers of these signs, whose messages focus entirely on the importance of environmental protection, reports that the majority of hotel guests who have the opportunity to participate in these programs do reuse their towels at least once during their stay. But could the results be improved?

Researchers are often on the lookout for ways to apply their scientific knowledge to make existing policies and practices even more effective. Much like a highway billboard that reads, "Place your ad here," these little towel recycling cards spoke to us, practically pleaded with us, to "Test your ideas here." So we did. And in doing so, we showed that just by making a small change to the way in which the request is made, hotel chains can do much, much better.

As this book will reveal, starting with our towel experiments, small, easy changes to our messages and to our requests can make them vastly more persuasive. In fact, we're going to claim that everyone's ability to persuade others can be improved by learning persuasion strategies that have been scientifically proven to be successful. We will report on dozens of studies, some conducted by us, some by other scientists, that demonstrate this point in many different settings. Along the way, we will discuss the principles behind these findings. The central purpose of this book is to provide the reader with a better understanding of the psychological processes underlying our efforts to influence others to shift their attitudes or behavior in a direction that results in positive outcomes for both parties. In addition to presenting a variety of effective and ethical persuasion strategies, we also discuss the types of things to watch out for to help you resist both subtle and overt influences on your decision-making.

The studies discussed in this book are scientifically rigorous, but they can also be fun. For example, we'll seek to provide insights about what single office supply can make your attempts to persuade others significantly more effective, what Luke Skywalker can teach us about being an influential leader, why people named Dennis are disproportionately more likely to become dentists, how slipping your audience the perfectly legal drug 1,3,7-trimethylxanthin can help you become more persuasive, how inconveniencing your rivals will make them more likely to do favors for you, and why people would be more likely to buy a BMW just after giving reasons for preferring a Mercedes.

We'll also seek to answer a number of other important questions. For example: What common mistake do communicators often make that causes their message to backfire? Which one word will strengthen your persuasion attempts? Is it better to start low or high when selling items on eBay? How can you turn your weaknesses into persuasive strengths? How can waiters increase their tips without changing the quality of their service? And why can sometimes seeing yourself—or being seen by others—as an expert result in one of the most dangerous situations in which you could ever be placed?

Persuasion as Science, Not Art

The scientific study of persuasion has been continuing for over half a century now. Yet, the research on persuasion is somewhat of a secret science, often lying dormant in the pages of academic journals. Considering the large body of research that's been produced on the subject, it might be useful to take a moment to think about why this research is so often overlooked. It's no surprise that people who are faced with choices about how to influence others, including important program or policy choices, will often base their decisions on thinking that's grounded in the established theories and practices of fields such as economics, finance, and public policy. However, what's puzzling is how frequently decision-makers fail to use established psychological theories and practices to guide them in their choices.

One potential explanation for this tendency is that, unlike the fields of economics, finance, and public policy, which tend to require learning from outsiders to achieve even a minimal level of competence, people believe they already possess an intuitive understanding of psychological principles simply by virtue of living life and interacting with others. As a consequence, they're less likely to learn and to consult the psychological research when making decisions, setting policies, or generating solutions to problems. This overconfidence inevitably leads people to miss golden opportunities for psychologically informed social influence—or worse still, to misuse psychological principles to the detriment of themselves and others.

Besides being overly reliant on their personal experiences with others, people also rely too much on introspection. For example, why would the marketing practitioners charged with the task of designing the hotel towel reuse signs focus almost exclusively on the impact of these programs on the environment? They probably did what any of us would do—they asked themselves, "What would motivate *me* to participate in one of these programs by recycling my towels?" And by examining their own motives, they would come to the conclusion that a sign that tapped into their values and identity as environmentally concerned people would be particularly motivating. But in doing so, they would also fail to realize how they could increase participation just by changing a few words in their request.

Persuasion has often been referred to as an art, but in a sense, this is a misclassification. Although talented artists can certainly be taught skills to harness their natural abilities, the truly remarkable artist seems to possess a certain level of talent and creativity that no instructor is capable of instilling in another person. Fortunately, this isn't the case with persuasion. Even people who consider themselves persuasion lightweights—people who feel they couldn't convince a child to play with toys—can learn to become persuasion heavyweights by understanding the psychology of persuasion and by using the specific persuasion strategies that have been scientifically proven to be effective.

Regardless of whether you're a salesperson, manager, marketer, negotiator, educator, policymaker, lawyer, health care worker, food server, eBayer, or parent, this book is designed to help you become a master persuader. We'll describe certain techniques that are based on what one of us (Robert Cialdini) explored in the book *Influence: Science & Practice* as the six universal principles of social influence: reciprocation (we feel obligated to return favors performed for us), authority (we look to experts to show us the way), commitment/consistency (we want to act consistently with our commitments and values), scarcity (the less available the resource, the more we want it), liking (the more we like people, the more we want to say yes to them), and social proof (we look to what others do to guide our behavior).[1] We'll discuss what these principles mean and how they operate in some detail throughout the book, but we won't limit ourselves to them. Although the six principles act as the foundation for the majority of successful social influence strategies, there are also many persuasion techniques that are based on other psychological factors, which we'll cover.

We'll also place a special emphasis on how these strategies operate in a number of different contexts—both within and outside the workplace—and provide practical and action-oriented advice for how to maximize your persuasive prowess in those settings and beyond. The advice we'll provide will be ethical and easy to follow, will require very little additional effort or cost on your part, and should pay big dividends.

With apologies to Henny Youngman, we fully expect that by the time you finish this book, your persuasion toolbox will be packed with so many scientifically proven social influence strategies you'll hardly be able to close it.

1

How can inconveniencing your audience increase your persuasiveness?

Colleen Szot is one of the most successful writers in the paid programming industry. And for good reason: In addition to penning several well-known "infomercials" for the famed and fast-selling NordicTrac exercise machine, she recently authored a program that shattered a nearly twenty-year sales record for a home-shopping channel. Although her programs retain many of the elements common to most infomercials, including flashy catchphrases, an unrealistically enthusiastic audience, and celebrity endorsements, Szot changed three words to a standard infomercial line that caused a huge increase in the number of people who purchased her product. Even more remarkable, these three words made it clear to potential customers that the process of ordering the product might well prove somewhat of a hassle. What were those three words, and how did they cause sales to skyrocket?

Szot changed the all-too-familiar call-to-action line,

"Operators are waiting, please call now," to, "If operators are busy, please call again." On the face of it, the change appears foolhardy. After all, the message seems to convey that potential customers might have to waste their time dialing and redialing the toll-free number until they finally reach a sales representative. Yet, that surface view underestimates the power of the principle of social proof: When people are uncertain about a course of action, they tend to look outside themselves and to other people around them to guide their decisions and actions. In the Colleen Szot example, consider the kind of mental image likely to be generated when you hear "operators are waiting": scores of bored phone representatives filing their nails, clipping their coupons, or twiddling their thumbs while they wait by their silent telephones—an image indicative of low demand and poor sales.

Now consider how your perception of the popularity of the product would change when you heard the phrase "if operators are busy, please call again." Instead of those bored, inactive representatives, you're probably imagining operators going from phone call to phone call without a break. In the case of the modified "if operators are busy, please call again" line, home viewers followed their perceptions of others' actions, even though those others were completely anonymous. After all, "if the phone lines are busy, then other people like me who are also watching this infomercial are calling, too."

Many classical findings in social psychology demonstrate the power of social proof to influence other people's actions. To take just one, in an experiment conducted by scientist Stanley Milgram and colleagues, an assistant of the researchers stopped on a busy New York City sidewalk and gazed skyward for sixty seconds. Most passersby simply walked around the man without even glancing to see what he was looking at. However, when the researchers added four other men to that group of sky gazers, the number of passersby who joined them more than quadrupled.[2]

Although there's little doubt that other people's behavior is a powerful source of social influence, when we ask people in our own studies whether other people's behavior influences their own, they are absolutely insistent that it does not. But social psychologists know better. We know that people's ability to understand the factors that affect their behavior is surprisingly poor.[3] Perhaps this is one reason that the people in the business of creating those little cards encouraging hotel guests to reuse their towels didn't think to use the principle of social proof to their advantage. In asking themselves, "What would motivate *me*?" they might well have discounted the very real influence that others would have on their behavior. As a result, they focused all their attention on how the towel reuse program would be relevant to saving the environment, a motivator that seemed, at least on the surface of it, to be most relevant to the desired behavior.

In our hotel experiment, we considered the finding that the majority of hotel guests who encounter the towel reuse signs do actually recycle their towels at least some time during their stay. What if we simply informed guests of this fact? Would it have any influence on their participation in the conservation program relative to the participation rates that a basic environmental appeal yields? With the cooperation of a hotel manager, two of us and another colleague created two signs and placed them in hotel rooms. One was designed to reflect the type of basic environmental-protection message adopted throughout much of the hotel industry. It asked the guests to help save the environment and to show their respect for nature by participating in the program. A second sign used the social proof information by informing guests that the majority of guests at the hotel recycled their towels at least once during the course of their stay. These signs were randomly assigned to the rooms in the hotel.

Now, typically, experimental social psychologists are fortunate enough to have a team of eager undergraduate research assistants to help collect the data. But, as you might imagine, neither our research assistants nor the guests would have been very pleased with the research assistants' sneaking into hotel bathrooms to collect our data, nor would our university's ethics board (nor our mothers, for that matter). Fortunately, the hotel's room attendants were kind enough to volunteer to collect the data for us. On the first day on which a particular guest's room was serviced, they simply recorded whether the guest chose to reuse at least one towel.

Guests who learned that the majority of other guests had reused their towels (the social proof appeal), which was a message that we've never seen employed by even a single hotel, were 26 percent more likely than those who saw the basic environmental protection message to recycle their towels.[4] That's a 26 percent increase in participation relative to the industry standard, which we achieved simply by changing *a few words* on the sign to convey what others were doing. Not a bad improvement for a factor that people say has no influence on them at all.

These findings show how being mindful of the true power of social proof can pay big dividends in your attempts to persuade others to take a desired course of action. Of course, the importance of how you communicate this information should not be underestimated. Your audience is obviously unlikely to respond favorably to a statement like, "Hey you: Be a sheep and join the herd. Baaaaaaaah!" Instead, a more positively framed statement, such as, "Join countless others in helping to save the environment," is likely to be received much more favorably.[5]

Besides the impact on public policy, social proof can have a major impact in your work life, as well. In addition to touting your top-selling products with impressive statistics conveying their popularity (think the McDonald's sign stating "Billions and billions served"), you'd do well to remember to always ask for testimonials from satisfied customers and clients. It's also important to feature those testimonials when you're presenting to new potential clients who may be in need of some reassurance about the benefits that your organization can provide. Or better yet, you can set up a situation in which your current clients have the opportunity to provide firsthand testimonials to prospective clients about how satisfied they are with you and your organization. One way to do this is to invite current and potential customers to a luncheon or educational seminar and arrange the seating charts so that they can easily commingle. In this setting, they're likely to naturally strike up conversations regarding the advantages of working with your organization. And if, while taking RSVPs for the luncheon, your potential attendees tell you they'll have to call you back to let you know, just be sure to tell them that if your phone line is busy, they should keep trying . . .

2

What shifts the bandwagon effect into another gear?

Herds are persuasive because people are motivated to follow other people's behavior. But *which* herds are people most likely to follow?

In the previous chapter, we noted that hotel guests followed the behavior of the herd of other hotel guests. But might people be even more influenced by a herd that looks even more like them—the herd of hotel guests who had previously stayed in *their particular room*? There are actually some good reasons to expect not. First, from a purely logical standpoint, you shouldn't exactly view the previous occupants of your hotel room in an especially positive light. After all, those are the same people who have, by simple virtue of staying in that room previously, played a larger role in reducing the quality of your room and its amenities than any other guests in the hotel, engaging in activities that range from the mundane to the who-knows-what. Second, there's no rational reason to believe that the behavior of those previously occupying your hotel room is any more valid than, say, the behavior of those previously occupying the room next door.

Yet, as we discussed, the psychological research shows that people are often wrong about what motivates them to engage in certain behavior.

The social proof message used in the hotel study informed guests that similar others—specifically, the majority of other guests who had previously stayed at the hotel—had reused their towels at least once during their stay. We decided to take the perceived similarity one step further by conducting another study in a hotel setting in which some hotel guests saw a request to reuse their towels communicating the social proof of guests who had specifically stayed in the *same room* in which they were staying. In addition to the standard environmental protection appeal and the social proof appeal used in the prior study, some guests saw a sign informing them that the majority of people who had previously stayed in their particular room participated in the towel reuse program at some point during their stay.

Guests who learned that the majority of the prior occupants of their particular room had participated were even more likely to reuse their towels than guests who learned the norms for the hotel in general. And compared to the standard environmental appeal, that was a 33 percent increase in the likelihood of participation.[6] These results suggest that if Henny Youngman had encountered a sign in his bathroom indicating that not a single person who had previously stayed in his room had ever stolen a towel, he probably would have had a much easier time closing his suitcase as he prepared to check out. But why?

It's usually beneficial for us to follow the behavioral

norms associated with the particular environment, situation, or circumstances that most closely match our own environment, situation, or circumstances.[7] For example, when you're at a public library, do you follow the norms of other library patrons, quietly browsing through the fiction section and occasionally whispering to your friends, or do you follow the norms of the patrons at your favorite bar, crushing books against your forehead on a dare and playing games where you take a drink from your flask every time you read a word with the letter "e"? If you want to avoid a lifetime ban from the premises, you'd obviously choose the former alternative rather than the latter.

Earlier, we described the importance of testimonials in trying to sway others' opinions in your direction. The results of this experiment suggest that the more similar the person giving the testimonial is to the new target audience, the more persuasive the message becomes. This means that in deciding which testimonials to show to a prospect, you need to take your ego out of the process. You should begin not with the testimonial you're most proud of, but with the one whose circumstances are most comparable to your audience's. For instance, a high-school teacher trying to convince a student to come to class more often should solicit comments about the benefits of doing so not from students in the front row, but rather from students who are more similar to the target student.

As another example, if you were selling software to the owner of a string of local beauty salons, she'd be more influenced by information about how pleased other salon owners are with your software than by how pleased the big shots at General Motors were. After all, she'd be likely to think, "If others *like me* have gotten good results with this product, then it should be right for me, too."

And if you're a leader or a manager attempting to persuade employees to willingly embrace a new system, you should ask for a positive testimonial from others within the same department who have already agreed to make the switch. But what if you've tried that, yet you still have one stubborn employee—perhaps the person who has been working with the older system the longest—whom you still can't win over? A common mistake managers might make in such a case would be to choose the most eloquent coworker to try to explain the benefits to his or her stubborn coworker, even if he or she is completely different from that person on a number of important dimensions. Instead, the manager's best bet would likely be to solicit the opinions of another coworker—perhaps someone else who had also been working under the system for a long time—even if that particular person happens to be somewhat less articulate or popular.

3

What common mistake causes messages to self-destruct?

Commercials are typically designed to move products, not people. But in the early 1970s, the Keep America Beautiful Organization created a commercial that was widely thought to be so moving that many consider it perhaps the most effective public service announcement of all time. Designed to infuse America's daily television-viewing diet with an extra serving of moral fiber, the spot featured a Native American reacting to the widespread corruption of the environment that he observed by shedding a single but powerful tear. Many years later, the same organization revisited its old friend in a new campaign designed to capture viewers' attention and reopen their tear ducts. This time, the camera featured several people waiting at a bus stop, engaging in everyday activities such as drinking coffee, reading the newspaper, and smoking cigarettes. After the bus arrived and they all climbed aboard, the camera cut to the empty bus stop waiting area, now completely covered with cups, newspapers, and cigarette butts. As the camera panned from right to left, it slowly zoomed in to a poster of the

Native American overlooking the littered bus stop, still with a tear in his eye. As the screen faded to black, the text of the spot's take-home message appeared: "Back by popular neglect."[8]

Back by *popular* neglect. What sort of message is conveyed by this phrase and by the litter-filled environments featured in this advertisement? It unintentionally conveys the message that despite strong disapproval for littering behavior, littering is quite common. Although communicating strong disapproval for the littering behavior might certainly prove motivating, conveying the fact that many people litter acts as strong social proof for more littering. Because people tend to follow the most popular course of action, this message can potentially be more harmful than helpful.

Other examples are abundant in everyday life. We don't mean to ruffle his feathers, but we take issue with some of the messages conveyed by the lovable but psychologically naïve U.S. Forest Service mascot, Woodsy Owl. In a long-running print ad titled "Gross National Product," he proclaims, "This year Americans will produce more litter and pollution than ever before." Several weeks before the 2004 presidential election, Women's Voices. Women Vote, a major political organization, sent out about 1 million mailings designed to increase participation in the political process by single women; their message was: "4 years ago, 22 million single women did not vote."[9] More generally, political groups of all sorts misunderstand the impact of their communications by condemning the rise in voter apathy and then watch their communications backfire as more and more voters fail to turn up at the polls. Health centers and hospitals place posters on waiting room walls decrying the number of patients who don't show up for their appointments; then they get frustrated when the nonattendance rates rise further. In Arizona, visitors to the state's Petrified Forest National Park quickly learn from prominent signage that the park's existence is threatened because so many visitors have been taking pieces of petrified wood from the grounds: "Your heritage is being vandalized every day by theft losses of petrified wood of 14 tons a year, mostly a small piece at a time."

Although these pronouncements and depictions may indeed reflect reality and are well intentioned, the designers of these campaigns may fail to realize that by using negative social proof as part of a rallying cry, they might be inadvertently focusing the audience on the prevalence, rather than the undesirability, of that behavior. In fact, we became aware of the wood theft problem at the Petrified Forest as a result of a story that a former graduate student told. He had visited the Petrified Forest with his fiancée–a woman he described as the most honest person he'd ever known, someone who had never borrowed a paper clip without returning it. They quickly encountered the aforementioned park sign warning visitors against stealing petrified wood. He was shocked when his otherwise wholly law-abiding fiancée nudged him in the side with her elbow and whispered, "We'd better get ours now."

To test the role of negative social proof (and to see if we could design a more effective message), one of us, along with a team of other scientists, created two signs designed

21

to deter wood theft at Petrified Forest National Park. The negative social proof sign said, "Many past visitors have removed the petrified wood from the park, changing the natural state of the Petrified Forest," and was accompanied by a picture of several park visitors taking pieces of wood. A second sign conveyed no social proof information. Rather, it simply conveyed that stealing wood was not appropriate or approved, saying, "Please don't remove the petrified wood from the park, in order to preserve the natural state of the Petrified Forest." That sign was accompanied by a picture of a lone visitor stealing a piece of wood, with a red circle-and-bar (the universal "No" symbol) superimposed over his hand. We also had a control condition in which we didn't put up either of these signs.

Unbeknownst to park visitors, we placed marked pieces of petrified wood along visitor pathways. We also varied what sign (if any) was posted at the entrance of each pathway. Through this procedure, we were able to observe how the different signs affected petrified wood theft.

In a finding that should petrify the National Park's management, compared with a no-sign control condition in which 2.92 percent of the pieces were stolen, the social proof message resulted in *more* theft (7.92 percent). In essence, it almost tripled theft. Thus, theirs was not a crime prevention strategy; it was a crime *promotion* strategy. In contrast, the other message, which simply asked visitors not to steal the wood and depicted a lone thief, resulted in slightly less theft (1.67 percent) than the control condition.[10]

Besides asking visitors not to steal the wood, the park management should have focused attention on the huge number of people who don't take any wood, to influence the few who do. This can often be done by simply reframing the statistics. For example, although fourteen tons of wood are stolen each year at the park, the actual number of thieves is minuscule (less than 3 percent of the visitor total) compared to the massive number of people who respect the park's rules and choose to preserve its natural resources.[11,12]

If the circumstances allow for it, focusing the audience on all people who do engage in the positive behavior can be a very influential strategy. For instance, imagine you are a manager recognizing that attendance at your monthly meetings has gone down. Rather than calling attention to the fact that so many people are missing the meetings, you could not only express your disapproval for that behavior, but also highlight that those who don't attend the meetings are in the minority by pointing out the large number of people who do actually turn up. Similarly, business leaders would be well advised to publish the number of departments, employees, or colleagues that have already incorporated a new software system, new procedures, or a new customer service plan into their everyday ways of working. In doing so, they can be assured that they are harnessing the power of social proof as opposed to having it potentially backfire on them by complaining about the many people who haven't come on board.

This strategy can be used to encourage many other types of socially desirable behavior. For instance, along with several colleagues, one of us created a set of three public service announcements designed to increase recycling in the state of Arizona. Each one included a scene in which the majority of the characters featured in the ad frequently recycled, and all spoke disapprovingly of a single person in the scene who did not recycle. This made it clear to the viewers that not only are people who don't recycle in the minority, but others widely disapprove of them and their behavior. The PSAs also included information about how to recycle and the benefits of doing so. For example, one purposely campy PSA featured a set of neighbors in a *Leave It to Beaver* type of scene, with several people standing on a driveway:

> **Child:** Over here, Mrs. Rodriguez, it's our week to take the recycling down to the center. [Child hands a paper bag filled with newspapers to his mother, who places it onto the flatbed of a truck. Mrs. Rodriguez does the same.]
> **Child:** Gee, Dad, where's Mr. Jenkins?
> [Mrs. Rodriguez rolls her eyes.]
> **Dad** [disappointed]: Well, son, you see, Mr. Jenkins doesn't recycle.

The camera then cut to a slovenly, unkempt Mr. Jenkins napping on a lawn chair in his backyard, completely enveloped by the old newspapers lying all around him. The camera then cut to the child's face, as a single tear rolled down his cheek.[*]

---

[*] Videos of the PSAs we created can be found at www.influenceatwork.com.

Finally, to emphasize the huge number of Arizonans who recycle, a picture of the geographical outline of the state of Arizona then appeared on the screen, filled with the faces of scores of different people, and the words "Arizona Recycles" accompanying the picture.

Typically, many veterans of the PSA industry will say their commercials have been successful if they are able to move 1 percent or 2 percent of the audience in the desired direction. These professionals commonly have the advantage of more experience, better equipment, and much greater access to funds than we had when making ours. Yet, in a field test in which this psychologically informed PSA and two others like it were played on local TV and radio stations of four Arizona communities, we recorded a 25.4 percent new advantage in recycling tonnage over a pair of control communities not exposed to the PSAs. All that on a budget so tight it would make a shoestring blush.

4

When persuasion might backfire, how do you avoid the magnetic middle?

The Petrified Forest study shows that people have a natural tendency to do what most other people are doing, even when that behavior is socially undesirable. Although we recommended trying to reframe the message to focus on the many people who are behaving in a more desirable way, unfortunately, that is not always possible. What's a persuader to do in those situations?

Consider a study two of us conducted with lead researcher Wes Schultz and several other colleagues. In this study, three-hundred California households agreed to have their weekly energy use recorded. Research assistants then went to participating homes and read their energy meters to get a baseline measure of how much energy the households consumed per week.* Afterward,

*For those concerned for the health of the meter readers, we should note that they performed the task during daylight hours and they weren't allowed to go into backyards with unchained dogs. So rest assured, no assistants were harmed in the making of this research.

a little card was hung on the front door of each household giving feedback to the homeowners about how their energy consumption compared to the neighborhood average. Of course, some of the households consumed more energy than the average, whereas others consumed less.[13]

Over the next several weeks, those who had been consuming more energy than their neighbors reduced their energy consumption by 5.7 percent. Not much of a surprise there. More interesting, however, was the finding that those who had been consuming *less* energy than their neighbors actually *increased* their energy consumption by 8.6 percent. These results show that what most others are doing acts as a "magnetic middle," meaning that people who deviate from the average tend to be drawn to the average like metal filings to a magnet—they change their actions to be more in line with the norm regardless of whether they were previously behaving in a socially desirable or a socially undesirable way.

So, how do we prevent the backfire effect that occurs when people already acting in a socially conscious way learn that they're deviating from the (less desirable) norm? It might be helpful to convey society's approval for their behavior in some way. But how? With the cost of singing telegrams prohibitively high these days, one less-expensive solution just might be to accompany the feedback with some sort of symbol of approval. Such an image would serve not only as a reminder of the desirability of energy conservation, but also as positive reinforcement. But what kind of symbol should we use? A thumbs-up image? An actual stamp of approval?

Yes!

How about a simple smiley face? To test this idea, another experimental condition was included in the study. For these other households, the feedback on the card was accompanied by either a smiley face ☺ or a frowny face ☹, depending, of course, on whether they were using more or less energy than the neighborhood average. The data revealed that the addition of the frowny face didn't make much of a difference. In other words, those who used a relatively large amount of electricity reduced their consumption by over 5 percent regardless of whether the feedback included the frowny face. We were quite impressed, however, by the impact of adding the smiley face to the feedback given to those who used a relatively small amount of electricity: Whereas their no-symbol peers had shown the 8.6 percent increase in energy consumption that we described earlier, these "smiley-faced" households continued to consume energy at the same low prefeedback rate.

The results of this study demonstrate not only the power of the social norm to bring people's behavior toward it like a powerful magnet, but also how we as persuaders can reduce the likelihood of our message backfiring for half of the population that receives it: We should convey our approval for, and appreciation of, those already acting in a socially desirable way.

Suppose, for example, that an internal report of a large company becomes public, and it states that the average employee arrives late for work 5.3 percent of the time. The good news is that those who arrive late more often than that will likely adjust their behavior to be more in line with the norm, but the bad news is that so will those who are much more consistently punctual. Our research shows that those who tend to come in on time should be praised for their behavior, and it should be made clear to them how much punctuality is appreciated.

Those who work in public services should also consider the impact of their messages. Although there may be rising rates of truancy in classrooms, school superintendents, teachers, and other education personnel should applaud and publicly declare the fact that the majority of parents see to it that their children do attend classes regularly, while also showing widespread disapproval for the small number of parents who don't. More generally, to prevent a good apple from getting spoiled by a bunch of bad ones, remember to show your appreciation for it.

5

When does offering people more
make them want less?

W e all know the feeling. We start a new job,
and immediately we're inundated with loads
of paperwork asking us to make all kinds of important
decisions. For many of us, one of those decisions is
whether to enroll in a retirement plan, in which part of
our salary is automatically placed in an investment fund
that we'll be able to access later in life. If we decide to
enroll, we're typically given many options from which
to choose so that we can find the one that's right for us.
However, despite the numerous incentives for enrolling
in these programs, which often include tax advantages
and matching employer contributions, many people
don't take advantage of them. But why? Could it be that
organizations are unknowingly discouraging enrollment
by offering their employees *too many* options?

Behavioral scientist Sheena Iyengar thinks so. She
and several colleagues analyzed company-sponsored
retirement programs for nearly eight hundred thousand
workers, looking at how the participation rates varied as
a function of how many fund choices the organization

offered. Sure enough, the researchers found that the more choices that were offered, the less likely the employees were to enroll in the program at all: For every ten additional funds a company offered to its employees, the participation rate dropped almost 2 percent. To give just one specific comparison, they found that when only two funds were offered, the rate of participation was roughly 75 percent, but when fifty-nine funds were offered, the participation rate dropped to about 60 percent.[14]

Iyengar and fellow social scientist Mark Lepper also examined whether the damaging effect of offering too much occurred in other domains, such as food products. They set up a display at an upscale supermarket in which passersby could sample a variety of jams that were all made by a single manufacturer. Throughout the course of the study, the researchers varied the number of flavors of the jam offered, so that either six or twenty-four flavors were featured at the display at any given time. The results demonstrated a clear and astonishing difference between the two conditions: Only 3 percent of those who approached the extensive-choice display actually purchased any jam. Contrast that with the 30 percent who bought jam when they approached the limited-choice display.[15]

What could possibly account for this tenfold increase in sales? When so many choices are made available, consumers often find the decision-making process frustrating, perhaps due to the burden of having to differentiate so many options from one another in an attempt to make the best decision. This may result in disengagement from the task at hand, leading to an overall reduction in motivation and interest in the product as a whole. The same logic holds for the retirement plans.

Does this mean that offering many varieties and alternatives is always a bad thing? Before trying to answer this question, let's first consider one of Vancouver's most celebrated sweet shops, La Casa Gelato. This business offers gelato, ice cream, and sorbetto in any flavor you could possibly think of—and many that you couldn't. What began as a sports and pizza bar in the Commercial District of Vancouver in 1982 has grown into what owner Vince Misceo describes as an "ice cream wonderland." Upon entering the store, customers are faced with an eclectic array of over two hundred flavors, including wild asparagus, fig and almond, aged balsamic vinegar, jalapeno, garlic, rosemary, dandelion, and curry.

Considering the research findings we discussed, has Vince Misceo, with his shop of over two hundred flavored gelatos, ice creams, and sorbettos, made a mistake by offering so many choices? The store's proprietor obviously embraces the philosophy that providing his customers with more choices will lead to better business, and it certainly appears from his success that he's right. For one thing, the extensive variety of flavors has generated a great deal of publicity for his business—the extremely varied offerings have become a unique, identifying feature of the brand. Second, the majority of his shop's clientele seem to genuinely savor—both literally and figuratively—the process of sampling and eventually choosing the flavors they would like to try. And third, maximizing the number of options available may be especially helpful when customers are likely to know exactly what they want and are simply looking for a store or a business that supplies it.

Unfortunately, there are few companies that find themselves in the position of having hordes of prospective buyers literally salivating at the opportunity to choose from their wide selection of goods and services. Instead, it's often the case that potential customers don't know precisely what they want until they've surveyed what's available to them. What this means for most businesses is that by saturating the market with a large number of unnecessary varieties of their products, they could well be inadvertently harming their sales, and as a result, they could be diminishing their profits. In such cases, a business might enhance a customer's motivation to purchase its goods and services by reviewing its product line and cutting out redundant or less-popular items.

There are a number of major manufacturers of a variety of consumer products that in recent years have been streamlining the range of options they provide to their customers, perhaps in response to a modest rebellion by their customers against the excessive number of choices they were offered. For example, take Procter & Gamble, a leading manufacturer of a wide range of products, from personal health care products and laundry detergents to prescription drugs. When the company reduced the number of versions of Head & Shoulders, one of its very popular shampoo products, from a staggering twenty-six to "only" fifteen, it quickly experienced a 10 percent increase in sales.[16]

What are the implications of these findings? Suppose that you work for an organization that sells many different variations of a similar product. Although it may seem against your intuition at first, it may be worth considering a reduction in the number of options provided by your business in order to drum up maximum interest in your offerings. This could be especially true if you have customers and clients who are uncertain of exactly what they might want. Of course, there could be additional benefits of offering less, such as making more storage space available, requiring reduced spending on raw materials, and a reduction in the production of marketing and point-of-sale materials to support a smaller portfolio. A worthwhile exercise would be to review the extent of your product portfolio and ask yourself the following question: Where we have customers who may not be clear about their requirements, might the number of choices we offer be causing them to seek other and potentially fewer alternatives elsewhere?[17]

The lessons of this research can also be applied to home life. Giving children choices in what books they'd like to read or what dinner they'd like to eat can undoubtedly be beneficial, but too many choices might be overwhelming and ultimately demotivating. The old saying may well assert that variety is the spice of life, but as the scientific research demonstrates, in some circumstances, too much variety, like too much spice, can be the ingredient that spoils the dish and, as a result, spoils your efforts at persuasion.

6

When does a bonus become an onus?

A stationery set. A ballpoint pen. A cosmetic case. A box of chocolates. A sample vial of perfume or cologne. An oil change. These are all examples of gifts or services offered free by companies, and chances are that at some point in your life as a consumer, you've been enticed by deals that offer products like these as gifts with your purchase of another product. Sometimes these little extras can be just the thing to push you to choose one company's product over another. But if everyone likes a gift, how could it be that giving gifts can actually backfire?

Social scientist Priya Raghubir wanted to test the idea that when consumers are offered a bonus gift for purchasing a product (the target product), the perceived value and desirability of the bonus gift as a standalone product can sharply decline. She thought this could be the case because consumers might infer that the product's manufacturer wouldn't give away a valuable product for free. In fact, it might even lead them to ask, "What might be wrong with this thing?" People may assume, for example, that the gift is obsolete or out of style, or perhaps that the supply overwhelmingly exceeded the demand and the manufacturer is simply trying to purge its inventory of the item. Or maybe they think it's just plain junk.

To test the idea that the value of an item declines when it's offered as a gift, Raghubir had participants view a duty-free catalog that featured liquor as the target product and a pearl bracelet as the bonus gift. One group of participants was asked to evaluate the desirability and value of the pearl bracelet in the context of the gift, and another group was asked to evaluate the pearl bracelet by itself. The results confirmed the hypothesis: People were willing to pay around 35 percent less for the pearl bracelet when they saw it bundled with the target product as an add-on than when they saw it as a standalone product.[18]

These findings reveal some potentially negative implications for businesses that promote a particular line of products by throwing in goods or services for free that the business normally sells independently. Raghubir suggests that one way of preventing the offer of gifts or services from backfiring is to inform or remind customers about the true value of the gift. For example, imagine that you work for a software company. One way that you attract new business is to offer a free piece of software, let's say a security program, to new customers. If in your advertising and your mailings you offer this free product and fail to point out what it would cost customers if they had to pay for it themselves, you're losing out on an effective way of positioning your offer as valuable and significant. After all, if you write down "free," numerically the number is $0.00—not a message you would want to send to prospective customers about the worth of your products. To ensure that your offer is seen as the valuable proposition it actually is, the customer needs to be shown the true value of your offer. So, no longer should your message read, "Receive a free security program." Instead, it becomes, "Receive a $250 security program at no cost to you."

The idea of valuing what you do doesn't just apply to those running a business. There are potential applications for anyone looking to influence others. You might point out to a colleague that you were happy to stay for an extra hour at work to help finish an important proposal because you know how much it means to his or her business prospects. You are valuing your time in your colleague's eyes, an entirely more influential strategy than simply saying nothing.

Similarly, if you are on the board of a school that's promoting a free after-school club for students, you would want to point out in the communication to parents what it would cost if those parents chose a private after-school students' club instead. In doing this, you create a value, which will likely increase the club's uptake of members as a consequence.

Not only do these findings have implications for business and public service transactions, they might work on your family as well. Perhaps you could use the results of this research to convince your in-laws that, in order to avoid having their opinions devalued, they should stop giving you free advice.

7

How can a new superior product mean more sales of an inferior one?

A number of years ago, the kitchen retail store Williams-Sonoma started offering a bread-making machine that was far superior to a best-selling bread maker that they stocked. Yet, when they added this new product to their inventory, sales of their existing best-seller nearly doubled. Why?

The story of Williams-Sonoma started during the late 1940s and early 1950s, when Chuck Williams, who worked as a contractor in Sonoma, California, traveled with a couple of his friends to Paris. There, they saw for the first time specialized French cooking equipment– omelet pans and soufflé molds whose quality and style he'd never seen in the United States. Voilà, the Williams Sonoma Kitchen Outlet was born. It grew quickly, opening more stores and starting a catalog business. A good portion of the sales from the catalog at one point came from the bread maker, whose sales nearly doubled immediately after an improved, more expensive one was introduced.

According to decision researcher Itamar Simonson, when consumers consider a particular set of choices for a product, they tend to favor alternatives that are "compromise choices"–choices that fall between what they need, at a minimum, and what they could possibly spend, at a maximum. When consumers must make a decision between two products, they often compromise by opting for the less-expensive version. However, if a third product were to be offered that was more expensive than the other two choices, the compromise choice would shift from the economy-priced product to the moderately priced product (which is no longer the highest-priced product in the set of choices). In the case of the Williams-Sonoma bread makers, the introduction of a more expensive bread maker made the original bread maker seem like a wiser and more economical choice in comparison.[19]

Let's say that you are a business owner or sales manager who has responsibility for the sale of a range of products and services. You would be well advised to recognize that your company's highest-end and highest-priced products provide two very important potential benefits for your business. The first is straightforward: These top-of-the-line products meet the high-end needs of a small group of current and future customers. As a result, you'll see greater revenues injected into your business by offering them. But the second is perhaps under-recognized: The next-highest-priced model will more likely be considered attractively priced, as a compromise.

Let's take an everyday example where this principle

is often not used to its full potential, an example that many of us will be familiar with—choosing a bottle of wine from a wine list in a bar or restaurant. A substantial number of wine bars and hotels will present their more expensive wines at the bottom of the wine list, though customers' eyes sometimes never even get there as they consider the many available options. In some establishments, the high-end champagnes might even be printed on a separate menu. As a result, the midrange wines and champagnes aren't presented as compromise choices and therefore they appear less attractive. Just by making a small change and offering these high-end wines and champagnes at the top of the menu, a restaurant should do much more business for its next-most-pricey alternative.

This strategy should be effective in a number of other domains. For example, suppose you were part of an organization that decided to pay for you to attend an educational conference taking place on a cruise ship, and that you wanted to stay in a room with a window. Rather than simply asking your manager his or her opinion about the window room, you can bookend that choice with two other possibilities—one that's not as nice (a windowless inside cabin) and one that's clearly better but may be viewed as too expensive (a room with a balcony). By constructing this set of alternatives around the window room, you increase the likelihood that he or she will agree that the alternative you desire is the best choice.

The compromise strategy doesn't just apply to bread makers, alcohol, and accommodations. Anyone who has a range of products or services to offer could make midrange products more popular by offering more expensive ones first. It's important to recognize that even if your company does employ this high-end framing approach, it could be that an unexpected slump in sales of the highest-end version of a product might tempt you to stop offering that item. However, as this research suggests, removing that item from the set of consumer choices without replacing it with another top-of-the-line product could produce a negative domino effect that would start with your next-highest-end version of your product and work its way down. Such a shift in your customers' compromise choice could land you in a compromising position of your own.

8

Does fear persuade or does it paralyze?

In his first inaugural address, the thirty-second U.S. president, Franklin Delano Roosevelt, uttered the following famous words to anxious, Depression-era Americans: "So, first of all, let me assert my firm belief that the only thing we have to fear is fear itself . . . which paralyzes needed efforts to convert retreat into advance." But was Roosevelt correct? When trying to persuade an audience to behave a certain way, does fear paralyze, as he suggested, or does it persuade and motivate?

For the most part, research has demonstrated that fear-arousing communications usually stimulate the audience to take action to reduce the threat. However, this general rule has one important exception: When the fear-producing message describes danger but the audience is not told of clear, specific, effective means of reducing the danger, they may deal with the fear by "blocking out" the message or denying that it applies to them. As a consequence, they may indeed be paralyzed into taking no action at all.

In one study conducted by health researcher Howard Leventhal and colleagues, students read a public health pamphlet detailing the dangers of tetanus infection. The pamphlet was either filled or not filled with frightening details of the consequences of contracting tetanus. In addition, they either did or did not receive a specific plan for how to arrange to get a tetanus injection. Finally, there was a control group of students who did not get a warning about tetanus but did get a plan of how to get a tetanus injection. The high-fear message motivated the participants to get a tetanus injection only if it included a plan identifying the specific action they could take to secure a tetanus injection and thereby reduce their fear of tetanus. The more clearly people see behavioral means for ridding themselves of fear, the less they will need to resort to denial.[20]

These findings can be applied to business and beyond. Advertising campaigns that inform potential customers of the real-world threats that a company's goods or services can alleviate should always be accompanied by clear, specific, effective steps they can take to reduce the danger. Simply scaring customers into believing that a product or service can help with a potential problem might have the opposite effect, potentially cementing them into inaction if there is a failure to provide specific, achievable steps that they can take to avoid such a threat.

Similarly, if you happen to spot a particularly serious problem in a large-scale project undertaken by your organization, you would be wise to accompany your statements to management with at least one viable plan of action the company could take to avert the potential disaster (assuming you can design a plan quickly, of course). If you decide that you will tell management about a problem first and generate a plan later, by the time you and your coworkers have developed a plan, management may have already found ways to block out the message or refuse to admit that it applies to that particular project.

Health care professionals and public service communicators should also be aware of the implications of this research. Physicians or nurses who wish to persuade an overweight patient to lose weight and exercise more often should focus that patient on the potential dangers of failing to lose weight, but only if they follow up that message with some clear, straightforward steps the patient can take to do so—perhaps in the form of a specific diet and a specific set of exercises. Simply pointing out that he or she is at an increased risk of cardiovascular disease and diabetes if no weight is lost might only serve to instill fear and denial in a patient. In the case of public service officials, merely painting a gruesome picture of the impact of dangerous behavior, such as smoking, having unprotected sex, and drunk driving, may also be ineffective—or even potentially backfire—if unaccompanied by a good plan of action.

Given the necessity of pairing a message conveying the potential threat faced by the audience with a clear, specific, easy-to-follow plan, perhaps Roosevelt's statement should be amended to say "the only thing we have to fear is fear *by* itself."

9

What can chess teach us about making persuasive moves?

In April 2005, despite facing strong censure by the United States government, the parliament of a sovereign nation voted overwhelmingly to grant citizenship to former world chess champion and then–fugitive from U.S. law enforcement Bobby Fischer. What country would risk straining its relationship with the world's most powerful nation to protect an eccentric outlaw who openly spoke highly of the September 11, 2001, hijackers? Was it Iran? Syria? North Korea?

Surprisingly, it was the nation of Iceland, typically a loyal ally of the United States. Of all the countries in the world, why would Iceland be so willing to welcome Bobby Fischer with open arms, especially considering he violated United Nations sanctions by playing a $5 million chess match in the former Yugoslavia?

The answer to this question requires us to go back over thirty years to a very high-profile chess match—the 1972 World Chess Championship match between challenger Fischer and the defending champion, the Russian master Boris Spassky. No match in the history of the game had received more world wide publicity and chess playing was given a tremendous impetus everywhere. The match, played at the height of the Cold War, has been dubbed the Chess Match of the Century.

Typical of his eccentricity, Fischer failed to arrive in Iceland for the opening ceremony. For several days, it looked doubtful that the match would be played at all, for it was proving impossible for the authorities to accommodate Fischer's myriad demands, such as banning television cameras and giving him a 30 percent share of the revenue from spectators. Fischer's behavior was full of self-contradictions, as it had been throughout his chess career and his personal life. Finally, after a surprise doubling of the prize fund and a great deal of persuasion, including a reputed phone call from then-U.S. secretary of state Henry Kissinger, Bobby Fischer did fly to Iceland—and went on to beat Spassky handily. By the time the contest had been completed, its coverage had been all over the pages of newspapers both domestic and foreign. Iceland was willing to tolerate Fischer's controversial persona because, in the words of one Icelandic news reporter on the BBC, "He put Iceland on the international map."[21]

Over thirty years later, Icelanders had not forgotten what a significant gift Fischer had bestowed upon the isolated nation. For instance, a representative in Iceland's foreign affairs ministry made a statement saying that Fischer "contributed to a rather special event here, over thirty years ago but that people remember very well." According to the BBC analysis, Icelanders were "keen to repay the favor by offering sanctuary to Mr. Fischer" even though many people considered Fischer to be unlikable on a personal level.

This event emphasizes the importance and universality of the norm of reciprocity, which obligates us to repay others for what we have received from them. The norm drives us toward fairness and equity in our everyday social interactions, our business dealings, and our close relationships, and it helps us build trust with others.

Social psychologist Dennis Regan conducted a classic study of reciprocation. In his experiment, people who received a small, unsolicited gift from a stranger in the form of a can of Coca-Cola purchased twice as many raffle tickets from him as those who received no gift at all. This occurred despite the fact that there was a time delay between the gift and the request, and the stranger didn't make any kind of reference to the original gift when he made his pitch about the raffle tickets.

Consistent with the relationship between Fischer and Iceland, Regan also found that those who received a can of Coke from the stranger made their purchase decisions completely irrespective of the extent to which they liked him. For the participants who had received the gift, those who didn't like him purchased just as many raffle tickets as those who did. This demonstrates that you don't necessarily have to be liked to receive the benefits of the reciprocation norm, you just have to be generous.[22]

That the norm of reciprocity has real staying power and transcends likability is a useful insight for anyone looking to be more persuasive. It should also be welcome news to anyone who is asked to do a large or costly favor for another person, for which there appears to be no short-term gain in sight. As informed and ethical influencers, we would be well advised to help out others or make concessions to them first. If we seek out and give our help to a team member, colleague, or acquaintance, we create a social obligation for that person to help us or support us at a future date. Offering help to our boss puts us in a cooperative light in his or her eyes that could serve us well when we need assistance. And the manager who offers to allow a member of his or her staff to leave the office a little early for a dentist appointment is a manager who has wisely invested in a colleague who will feel the need to reciprocate that gesture in the future if an important project needs to be completed.

President John F. Kennedy once famously said, "Ask not what your country can do for you. Ask what you can do for your country." From an interpersonal standpoint, there may be no better orientation for those who wish to be influential among friends, coworkers, and customers. We often make the mistake of asking, *"Who can help me here?"* This may be a shortsighted approach to influencing others. It is far more productive to ask ourselves, *"Whom can I help?"* or, *"For whom can I do a favor?"* If management is about getting things done through others, then a healthy web of indebted colleagues, who have benefited from a manager's useful information, concessions, attention, and perhaps a friendly listening ear, can stand that manager in good stead for the future. Similarly, our friends, neighbors, and partners will become more responsive to our requests when we have first provided for them.

We should also note that there's one particular type of

person for whom a little favor goes a long way—customer service agents. If you've ever had a problem with your computer, tried to make a last-minute change to a plane ticket, or wanted to return an item to a vendor, you've probably encountered a less-than-helpful customer service agent at one point or another. To reduce the likelihood that you'll have such an encounter, try the following: If you find toward the beginning of your interaction that the customer service agent is being particularly friendly, polite, or responsive—perhaps before you get to your toughest request—tell the agent that you're so happy with the service so far that you're going to write a positive letter or email about your interaction to his or her supervisor as soon as you get off the phone. After getting the agent's name and the supervisor's contact information, you can then get to the more complex issues at hand. (Or, even easier, you can tell the person that you're so happy with the service that you'd like to be transferred to the agent's supervisor when you are done so that you can pay the person a compliment.) Although there are several psychological reasons for why this might be an effective strategy, the norm of reciprocity is a powerful factor here: You've offered to do a favor for that person, so now that person is going to feel obligated to return the favor. And, for the low cost of paying a quick compliment afterward, you can avoid getting into a strategic chess match—and perhaps a screaming match—with the agent that may ultimately lead to disappointment and frustration. So long as you follow through with your promise, the strategy should be an ethical and effective one.

10

Which office item can make your influence stick?

Paper clips, pens, pencils, pads, protractors, planners, and paperweights. Your office desk is full of practical items. But is there one common office item that can help make your influence attempts stick?

Social scientist Randy Garner wondered whether sticky notes, the best-known being Post-it Notes, made by the 3M Corp., might have the power to enhance compliance with a written request made to another person. In an intriguing study, he sent out surveys to people with a request to complete them. The survey was accompanied by either (a) a handwritten sticky note requesting completion of the survey, which was attached to a cover letter; (b) a similar handwritten message on the cover letter; or (c) the cover letter and survey alone.

That little yellow square packed quite a persuasive punch: More than 75 percent of the people who received the survey with the sticky note request filled it out and returned it, whereas only 48 percent of the second group and 36 percent of the third group did so. Why was it so successful? Could it be the simple fact that sticky notes are attention-grabbing in all their neon glory?

To test this possibility, Garner sent out a new batch of surveys. This time, a third of the surveys came with a Post-it Note with a handwritten request, a third came with a blank Post-it Note, and a third had no Post-it Note at all. If the benefits of using sticky notes come mainly from their ability to attract attention, then response rates should be equally high for both sets of Post-it Note surveys. That turns out not to be the case, however. The handwritten sticky note outperformed its competition, with a response rate of 69 percent compared to 43 percent for the surveys with the blank sticky note and 34 percent for the surveys with no sticky note.

So what's the explanation? Although finding a Post-it Note, slapping it on a cover sheet, and handwriting a message on it isn't exactly the most difficult of tasks, Garner suggests that people recognize the extra effort and personal touch that this requires, and that they feel the need to reciprocate this personal touch by agreeing to the request. After all, reciprocity is the social glue that helps bring and keep people together in cooperative relationships—and you can bet that it's a stronger adhesive than the kind on the back of a sticky note.

The evidence supports this reciprocity-based explanation. Garner found that placing a personalized sticky note on the survey did more than just simply persuade people to respond to the survey at higher rates: Those who filled out the survey with the handwritten sticky note message returned it more promptly and gave more effortful, detailed, and attentive answers to the questions. In fact, when the researcher made the note even more personal in nature by adding his initials and "Thank You!" to the handwritten message, the response rate shot up even higher.[23]

Broadly speaking, this research provides a valuable insight into human behavior: An ounce of personalized extra effort is worth a pound of persuasion. The more personalized you make a request, the more likely you'll be to get someone to agree to that request. More specifically, this research shows that in the office or in the community, a personalized sticky note could highlight the importance of your reports and communications and prevent them from becoming the proverbial needle in a haystack of other reports, letters, and mailings that are also vying for attention. What's more, the timeliness and quality of compliance with your request are likely to be enhanced as well.

What's the bottom line? If you use personalized messages for your persuasive practices, the 3M Corp. won't be the only ones posting a profit.

11

Why should restaurants ditch their baskets of mints?

Unless you're on your way to slay a vampire, after a garlicky meal at a restaurant, you're probably hoping to see a basket of mints by the exit. Yet, could it be that offering the mints in this location might not be the sweetest arrangement for the restaurant and its wait staff?

Although many restaurants have the mints placed in a basket near the door, some provide the mints in a different and far more effective way. At these restaurants, diners will be given a little gift at the end of their meal by their food servers. In the majority of cases, it's nothing more than a chocolate, mint, or other type of candy presented on a silver platter along with the bill.

Behavioral scientist David Strohmetz and colleagues conducted an experiment to determine what effect, if any, giving a little candy to patrons at the end of the meal would have on food servers' tips. In one set of trials, when presenting the bill, the food servers included a single piece of candy for each diner sitting at the table. Compared to occasions on which diners received no candy, the researchers found a modest increase in tips—not a huge one, just 3.3 percent. In a second set of trials, the food servers gave two candies to each diner at the table—and tips rose by 14.1 percent compared to the no-candy condition. All of this is reasonably predictable, considering what we know about the norm of reciprocity—the more a person gives to us, the more we feel obligated to give in return. But what factors make a gift or favor most persuasive? It turns out that the third condition in this study provides us with the answer.

For the third group of diners, the servers first gave one piece of candy to each person at the table. They then turned away from the table, signaling that they were leaving. However, before exiting the area completely, they turned back toward the diners at the table, reached into a pocket, and placed a second piece of candy on the table for each diner. Through this gesture, it was almost as if they were saying to the customers, " . . . oh, for you nice people, here is an extra candy each." The result? A 23 percent increase in tips.[24]

This study demonstrates that there are three major factors that help make a gift or favor more persuasive and as a result more likely to be reciprocated. The first is *significance*. Giving diners two candies compared to one had the effect of increasing tips from 3.3 percent to over 14 percent because two seemed significant, where one seemed pro forma. Notice that significant need not mean costly. Two candies cost no more than a few pennies. But also notice the difference between the two multiple-candy conditions. There was no difference in the *amount* of gift given, but there was a difference in the *way* the gift was given. When the server gave the diners an extra candy, their gift was *unexpected* and *personalized*. The diners in this third set of trials probably concluded that after they were given the one candy and the waiter turned away, this would be the last interaction they would have with him—and that's exactly why the gift was unexpected. By making it seem as if he felt a special liking for that table's diners in particular, the gift of the second candy appeared to be quite personalized.

This research clearly shows the value of giving gifts that are significant, unexpected, and personalized. Of course, if servers used this tactic on every table, not only would they be seen as unethical by the restaurant patrons, the tactic wouldn't work for long. As soon as diners noticed that the same practice was being used on everyone, the value of the gift would collapse—it wouldn't be seen as possessing any of these three important factors. Instead, it would be viewed as a cunning trick, and it would backfire. However, it is possible to use the lessons of the study in an ethical manner. To ensure that any gift that you give or favor that you perform is most appreciated, make sure to take some time to find out what gift, to the recipient, would best fit those three important criteria.

Even if we consider only the findings from the first two conditions of the study, however, we can see that a restaurant that chooses to put its mints by the exit may be missing out on an important opportunity to have the food servers give a token of appreciation to their patrons and receive a token of appreciation from their patrons in return. Even though the cost of these little candies may only be a few pennies, the diners' appreciation of the restaurant's efforts will be invaluable.

12

What's the pull of having no strings attached?

What's one of the best ways to secure someone's cooperation to work toward a common goal? Earlier we talked about how most hotels that have towel reuse programs try to persuade their guests to cooperate with them by reminding the guests about the importance of protecting the environment. Some hotels, however, take an additional step toward creating a cooperative atmosphere: They offer guests an incentive for their cooperation. In these incentive-based messages, the towel reuse card indicates that if the guests reuse their towels, the hotel will donate a percentage of the energy savings to a nonprofit environmental protection organization.

It's easy to imagine why the designers of these signs would think that incentives would be effective. Most of us intuitively believe that incentives work: Ice cream cones excel at persuading kids to clean their rooms, carefully timed treats can help even old dogs learn new tricks, and paychecks are quite good at limiting the number of times we hit the snooze button before getting out of bed and going to work each morning. Although the incentives being offered would not directly benefit the guests, it still seems logical that guests would be especially motivated to participate in the program because of the additional benefit to the environment being offered by the hotel. But does it work?

To find out, two of us conducted another study at the same local hotel. This time, some rooms displayed towel reuse cards that featured the standard environmental appeal, whereas other rooms displayed cards using this incentive-based approach. When we examined the data, we found that this new persuasive appeal produced no improvement over the standard environmental protection sign. Why?

There was good reason to believe that a small shift needed to occur in that message to make it more persuasive than the standard approach. After all, there's little social obligation to cooperate with someone who offers you something only on the condition that you initiate the cooperative effort. That kind of exchange is simply an economic transaction. On the other hand, there's a powerful sense of obligation, embodied in the norm of reciprocation, to return favors already performed for you. Little wonder, then, that the incentive-based cooperation appeal was no more effective in persuading the guests to reuse their towels than the standard appeal—it contained no social obligation to comply with the request, as the hotel gave nothing first.

This suggests that the hotels using the incentive-based cards may have gotten the general idea of cooperation right, but gotten the sequence wrong. Considering our knowledge of how the norm of reciprocity operates, perhaps a more effective way to increase participation in the program would be to reverse the sequence of favor-doing—in other words, for the hotel to *give the donation first* with no strings attached, *then* ask guests to cooperate in this effort by reusing their towels. This idea formed the basis for a third message that we also included in that study.

This third message was similar to the incentive-based message in that it discussed a donation to a nonprofit environmental protection organization. However, rather than offering to make the donation only on the condition that the guests took the first step in the cooperative effort, this appeal stated that the hotel *had already donated* to such an organization—and it did so *on behalf of its guests*. It then asked the guests to reciprocate this gesture by reusing their towels during their stay.

Impressively, those who saw the reciprocation-based message were 45 percent more likely to reuse their towels than those who saw the incentive-based message. This finding is particularly interesting in light of the fact that these appeals have nearly the same content. Although both of these messages informed the guests that the hotel was donating money to a nonprofit environmental protection agency, the reciprocation-based message informed the guests that the hotel had initiated the joint effort, using the forces of reciprocation and social obligation to prompt guests to participate in the program.[25]

Along with data from other research studies, these findings make it clear that when we're trying to solicit cooperation from other people—be they coworkers, clients, students, or acquaintances—we should offer help to them in a way that's unconditional and no-strings-attached. Approaching the potentially cooperative relationship in this way should not only increase the likelihood that you'll secure their cooperation in the first place, but also ensure that the cooperation you do receive is built on a solid foundation of trust and mutual appreciation, rather than on a much weaker incentive system. You'll also find this approach to be much longer lasting. Otherwise, the moment the incentive you've been promising or awarding can no longer be offered or is no longer desired by the other person, the brittle foundation of the relationship may crack, and the cooperative bridge you've built up may come crashing down.

13

Do favors behave like bread or like wine?

I n several of the previous chapters, we sought to offer evidence that by first providing a gift, service, or favor for someone, we create a social obligation in the recipient to reciprocate at a future date. Whether that gift consists of providing some useful information, helping out a colleague with a favor, placing a personalized sticky note on a request we make to others, or in the case of Bobby Fischer, putting a whole country on the map, there is a social obligation to repay others the form of behavior they have afforded to us. But what happens to the influence of those gifts and favors as time passes? Are favors like bread in that they become stale over time? Or are they more like wine, getting better and increasing in value with age? According to researcher Francis Flynn, the answer to this question depends on whether you are the favor-doer or favor-receiver.

Flynn asserts that immediately after one person performs a favor for another, the recipient of the favor places more value on the favor than does the favor-doer. However, as time passes, the value of the favor decreases in the recipient's eyes, whereas for the favor-doer, it actually increases. Although there are several potential reasons for this discrepancy, one possibility is that, as time goes by, the memory of the favor-doing event gets distorted, and since people have the desire to see themselves in the best possible light, receivers may think they didn't need all that much help at the time, while givers may think they really went out of their way for the receiver.

To test this idea, Flynn conducted a survey of employees working in the customer service department of a large U.S. airline. This particular business context is one in which coworkers commonly exchange favors by helping one another to cover shifts. The researcher asked half of the employees to consider a time when they had performed a favor for a coworker, whereas the other half of the employees were asked to consider a time when they had received a favor. All the employees in the study were then asked to indicate the perceived value of the favor and also to specify how long ago the favor was performed. Consistent with Flynn's hypothesis, the results of the survey revealed that recipients of the favor perceived it as more valuable immediately after the favor was performed but less valuable as time passed. Favor-doers, on the other hand, showed just the opposite effect: They placed a lower value on the favor immediately after it was performed but then placed greater value on it as time went by.[26]

These findings have implications for our effectiveness in persuading others both inside and outside the workplace. If you've done a favor for a colleague or an acquaintance, that favor will likely have the most impact on that person's desire to reciprocate within a short period of time following the favor. However, if you're the recipient of a favor, you need to be aware of the tendency of people in your position to downplay that favor as time goes by. If you fail to recognize the full value of the favor weeks, months, or even years after it has occurred—which Flynn's research shows is a natural inclination—this may ultimately damage your relationship with the favor-doer. If you are the giver of the favor, you might tend to think ill of the recipient due to his or her reticence to pay back what you have given previously.

So what can be done to maximize the value of a favor we provide if its value might diminish in the eyes of the receiver over time? One way might be to recognize the value of the gift or favor you have provided at the time by telling the receiver that you were happy to help because you know "that if the situation was ever reversed, I'm sure that you would do the same for me."

A second and potentially more risky strategy might be to restate the value of the previous gift before making a subsequent request in the future. Of course, you should consider carefully the words you choose when taking this approach. Saying something like, "Remember when I helped you out a few weeks ago? Well, now it's payback time!" is destined to fail. But offering a gentle reminder, perhaps by enquiring, "How useful did you find the report I sent to you?" might be an appropriate communication before you make your request.

Although there's no universal method of influencing others 100 percent of the time, we're certain that understanding all the factors that influence favor valuation is a good start. And if all else fails, just remember one simple rule of favor exchange: Just as you'll catch more flies with honey than with vinegar, you'll definitely catch more favors with a bottle of vintage wine than with a loaf of stale old bread.

14

How can one small step help your influence take a giant leap?

Imagine that your house is situated in a wealthy, picturesque community—the kind of neighborhood where people take great pride in perfectly trimmed hedges, uniformly colored grass, and freshly painted white picket fences. One day, someone from the local Road Traffic Safety Committee knocks on your door and asks if you'd be willing to support the Drive Carefully Through Our Neighborhood campaign by placing a large, unsightly sign measuring six feet by three feet and stating DRIVE CAREFULLY on your front lawn. His assurance that workmen, and not you, will be employed to dig the support holes in which the billboard posts will be placed does little to ease your concerns.

How many people do you think would agree to such a request? According to an experiment conducted by social psychologists Jonathan Freedman and Scott Fraser, 17 percent of homeowners in a posh neighborhood agreed to it. But astonishingly, the researchers were able to obtain a 76 percent compliance rate from a different set of residents from the same neighborhood simply by making one seemingly insignificant addition to their request. What was the addition, and what does that tell us about how to persuade others effectively?

A different research assistant approached this separate group of residents two weeks prior to this burdensome request and asked them if they'd be willing to display a very small, relatively inconspicuous sign in their window that read BE A SAFE DRIVER. Because it was such a small request, almost all of these residents agreed. Two weeks later, when someone else came to their home and asked them if they'd be willing to place the large billboard on their otherwise perfectly manicured lawn, they were much more inclined to agree.

But why would such a simple additional request, a strategy that the researchers refer to as the "foot-in-the-door technique," result in this astonishing boost in compliance with the much larger request? The evidence suggests that after agreeing to the request, the residents came to see themselves as committed to worthy causes, such as safe driving. When these homeowners were approached a couple of weeks later, they were motivated to act consistently with this perception of themselves as concerned citizens.[27]

There are countless applications of the foot-in-the-door technique, including sales applications. For example, one astute sales expert advises, "The general idea is to pave the way for full-line distribution by starting with a small order. . . . Look at it this way—when a person has signed an order for your merchandise, even though the profit is so small it hardly compensates for the time and effort of making the call, [he or she] is no longer a prospect–[he or she] is a customer."[28]

In cases in which a business can't secure even a small initial product purchase, this commitment- and consistency-based strategy has other uses. For example, potential clients who are reluctant to use your service may be more inclined to do so if they're first asked to take a small step, such as agreeing to an initial ten-minute appointment.

Similarly, a marketing research department is more likely to get people to answer a large number of survey questions by first asking them if they'd be willing to answer a brief survey. In fact, Freedman and Fraser conducted another experiment supporting this last point. In that experiment, a research assistant called up homeowners and asked them if they'd be willing to participate in a survey. Specifically, the caller said:

> The survey will involve five or six men from our staff coming into your home some morning for about 2 hours to enumerate and classify all the household products that you have. They will have to have full freedom in your house to go through the cupboards and storage places. Then all this information will be used in the writing of the reports for our public service publication, "The Guide."

In response to this very inconvenient request, 22 percent of the homeowners agreed–pretty amazing, considering that behavior this intrusive usually requires a search warrant.

However, the researchers called a second set of residents three days before this invasive request. In the first call, they were asked:

> We are calling you this morning to ask if you would answer a number of questions about what household products you use so that we could have this information for our public service publication, "The Guide." Would you be willing to give us this information for our survey?

Most agreed. Sure enough, three days later, nearly 53 percent of these homeowners agreed to the larger request.

Such an approach can also be applied to two of the most resistant influence targets that you're ever likely to come across—your children and yourself. Resistant children who easily find excuses not to do their homework or tidy their room are more likely to be persuaded if they're first asked to take a small step in that direction. This could take the form of asking them to spend a short period of time with you working on their homework or requesting that they put a cherished toy back in its box when they've finished playing with it. As long as they feel they've said yes to the first small request voluntarily—rather than through coercion—the psychological momentum should propel them toward scholastic awards and cleaner living quarters in which to place those awards.

In the case of influencing ourselves, rather than setting a large and seemingly insurmountable goal to improve, for example, our fitness levels, we would be well advised to set a task for ourselves that is small enough that we would have no excuse for not completing it at least once—for example, taking a short walk around the block. As a result, we should find ourselves gradually increasing our degree of commitment to meet the larger fitness goals. After all, Confucius wisely said, "A journey of a thousand miles begins with a single step."

15

How can you become a
Jedi master of persuasion?

A long time ago (about a quarter-century ago, to be
exact), in a galaxy far, far away, Luke Skywalker
gained the ultimate form of compliance: He persuaded
Darth Vader to turn against the evil emperor, saving his
own life and restoring hope and peace to the rest of the
galaxy. What social influence strategy did he use?

The movie *Return of the Jedi,* the final episode of the
Star Wars series, includes a scene in which Luke Skywalker turns to Darth Vader and says, "I know there's
still good in you. There's good in you, I can sense it."
Is it possible that these simple words could have persuaded Vader—or at the very least, planted the seeds of
persuasion—to come over to the Light Side of the Force
when Luke asked Vader to save him from the emperor?
According to the social psychological research, the
answer appears to be yes.

This strategy, known as the labeling technique,
involves assigning a trait, attitude, belief, or other label
to a person, and then making a request of that person
consistent with that label. In an effective demonstra-

tion of this strategy, researchers Alice Tybout and Richard Yalch showed how the labeling technique could be used to increase the likelihood that people would vote on Election Day. They interviewed a large number of potential voters and randomly told half of them that, based on their responses, they could be characterized as "above-average citizens likely to vote and participate in political events." The other half of the interviewees were informed that they could be characterized as about average in terms of these interests, beliefs, and behaviors. Those respondents given the label of good citizen, with a high likelihood of voting, not only came to see themselves as better citizens than those labeled as average, but they also were 15 percent more likely to vote in an election held one week later.[29]

Of course, the labeling technique isn't limited to political change in democracies or the Empire. There are a number of ways that you can use this technique in your business dealings and other personal interactions. For example, let's say that someone in your work team is struggling with a particular project you have asked him to manage. Perhaps this team member is losing confidence in his ability to provide the required deliverables of the project. A useful approach, assuming that you still believe him to be capable of the task, would be to remind him how hardworking and persevering he is. You should even point out examples of previous times when he had triumphed over similar challenges and successfully delivered. Teachers, trainers, and parents can apply this labeling strategy to sculpt desired behavior by pointing out that they regard their students, clients, or children as just the type of people who would thrive when given this sort of challenge. This strategy works for adults and children alike. For instance, research one of us conducted with several colleagues showed that when teachers tell children that they seem like the kind of students who care about having good handwriting, the kids spent more of their free time practicing their handwriting—even when they thought no one was around to watch.[30]

A company's relationship with its clients can be strengthened in this way. You might be familiar with the way many of the airlines have taken advantage of this principle: When the chief flight attendant tells a plane's passengers at the end of the flight, "We know you have many airlines to choose from, so we thank you for choosing ours," he or she is using a derivative of the labeling technique, reminding you implicitly that if there are so many choices out there, you must have chosen this airline for a reason. Told that they have confidence in that airline, passengers come to believe it. Similarly, you can use the technique to remind clients that their decision to deal with your organization shows their confidence in your company and in you, and that you appreciate and will continue to justify that confidence.

Just remember, as tempting as it might be to move over to the Dark Side with this strategy, like all other influence strategies, this one must be used only earnestly—in other words, only when the trait, attitude, belief, or other label accurately reflects the audience's natural capabilities, experiences, or personality. Of course, we know you wouldn't even think of using this strategy in an insincere manner. After all, we sense much good in you.

71

16

How can a simple question drastically increase support for you and your ideas?

A s any politician will tell you, in election periods, candidates are under enormous pressure to find ways not only to convince the electorate that they are the most qualified and credible leader, but also to draw those supporters to the polls on Election Day to secure their votes. Whereas some campaigners will invariably pour more and more money into television advertisements, mailings, and media appearances, the truly astute candidate—and probably the winning candidate—will look to harness not just the art of persuasion, but the science as well.

The 2000 U.S. presidential election, in which only 537 votes made a huge difference, made it clearer than ever before that every single vote really does count. During that infamous election, with the media and the United States as a whole focused on myriad controversies, one important fact was that even the tiniest boost in voter turnout in one direction or the other could have had a large impact on the outcome. What simple strategy could have been used to draw supporters from either side to the polls?

The answer involves merely asking potential voters to predict whether they will vote on Election Day and to provide a reason for their prediction. When social scientist Anthony Greenwald and his colleagues tried this technique on potential voters on the eve of one such Election Day, those who were asked to make a prediction yielded a turnout rate that was twenty-five percentage points higher than the rate for those who weren't asked (86.7 percent compared to 61.5 percent).[31]

There are two important psychological steps involved in the success of this technique. First, when people are asked to predict whether they'll engage in a socially desirable behavior in the future, they feel compelled to say yes because that's the socially desirable thing to say. Considering the value that society places on voting, it'd be difficult for the respondents to say something like, "Voting? That's this Tuesday, right? Can't do it. There's a really important History Channel special on civic responsibility that I don't want to miss." It's no surprise, then, that in this study, 100 percent of all the survey respondents asked to make a prediction about their voting behavior claimed that they would indeed vote.

Second, after most (if not all) of these people have publicly stated that they'll perform the socially desirable behavior, they'll be motivated to behave consistently with the commitment they just made. For instance, one restaurant owner greatly reduced the percentage of no-shows (people who booked a table but didn't honor the reservation and didn't call to cancel it) by having his receptionist change what she said when taking a reservation from, "Please call if you have to cancel," to, "Will you please call if you have to cancel?" Of course, nearly all customers committed themselves to calling by saying "yes" to that question. More important, they then felt the need to be consistent with their commitment: The no-show rate dropped from 30 percent to 10 percent.

Consequently, an easy way for candidates to get more of their supporters to the polls is to have volunteers call these self-proclaimed supporters, ask them if they'll vote in the next election, and wait for the "yes." If the caller then adds, "We'll mark you down as a 'yes' and I'll let the others know as well," the commitment has three components that potentially cement that potential voter's commitment: The commitment becomes voluntary, active, and publicly declared to others.

What lessons can we draw from this research that you can employ effectively in the workplace and in the broader community? Let's say that you're thinking about doing a charity run for your favorite nonprofit organization, but you don't want to sign up unless you are fairly certain you'll get a lot of donations. Asking family, friends, and coworkers whether they think they'll donate will not only give you an idea of their initial support for your undertaking, but will also increase the likelihood they will donate should you decide to join the run. As another example of this strategy, imagine that you manage a team of people and you recognize that the success of a new initiative depends not just on gaining verbal support from others on your team, but also on turning that verbal support into meaningful action. Rather than just explaining to team members what benefits they would derive from supporting a particular initiative, you would be well advised to also ask them if they would be willing to support such an initiative and wait for a "yes" in response. Following that yes response, you should ask those coworkers and colleagues to describe briefly why they support the initiative.

17

What is the active ingredient in lasting commitments?

The Amway Corporation, one of America's most profitable direct-selling companies, encourages its sales personnel by providing the following advice:

> One final tip before you get started: Set a goal and write it down. Whatever the goal, the important thing is that you set it, so you've got something for which to aim—and that you write it down. There is something magical about writing things down. So set a goal and write it down. When you reach that goal, set another and write that down. You'll be off and running.[32]

Why might writing down our goals be so effective at strengthening our commitments?

Put simply, commitments that are made actively have more staying power than those that are made passively. In a recent demonstration of both the power and subtlety of active commitments, social scientists Delia Cioffi and Randy Garner solicited college student volunteers for an AIDS education project to be carried out at local schools.

The researchers set up the study so that the students were given one of two different sets of instructions. Those who received the active instructions were told that if they wanted to volunteer, they should fill out a form stating that they were willing to participate. In contrast, those who received the passive instructions were told that if they wanted to volunteer, they should leave blank the form stating that they were not willing to participate.

The researchers found that the percentage of people who agreed to volunteer didn't differ as a function of whether the instructions invited active or passive responding. Yet there was quite an astonishing difference in the percentage of people who actually showed up to participate in the project several days later. Of those who agreed to participate passively, only 17 percent actually appeared as promised. What about those who agreed to participate through active means? Of those, 49 percent kept their promises. In all, the clear majority of those who appeared as scheduled (74 percent) were those who had actively agreed to volunteer for the program.[33]

Why are commitments that are written (and therefore active) so much more successful at eliciting participation? People make judgments about themselves based on observations of their own behavior, and they infer more about themselves based on their actions than on their nonactions. In support of this explanation, Cioffi and Garner found that those who volunteered actively were more likely to attribute their decisions to their own personality traits, preferences, and ideals than were those who volunteered passively.

What can active commitments do for you? Let's say

that it is the time of year when many of us traditionally make a very specific commitment—the "New Year's Resolution." Writing down and describing in detail the resolution you have committed to, rather than just thinking about it, and also describing what steps you will take to achieve your chosen commitment, could be helpful to you, especially if you then go on to show your friends and family those written commitments.

If you're a sales manager, asking members of your sales team to write down their goals will help strengthen their commitment to those goals and ultimately boost everyone's bottom line. It would also be wise to ensure that, during a meeting, participants write down and publicly share the actions that they have agreed to take.

A similar example in the retail environment also provides a telling illustration of the power of actively writing things down. Many stores offer their customers the opportunity to spread the cost of purchasing products over a number of months or even years by signing up for a store credit card or some other finance product. Retailers find that customers are less likely to cancel the agreement if the customers themselves, rather than the salesperson, fill out the application form. These data show that to maximize commitments to the initiatives you undertake jointly with clients and business associates, you should arrange for all parties involved to take an active role filling out any relevant business agreements.

Active commitments also have the potential to be used with great benefit throughout the health care industry. In recent years, health care providers have reported that more patients than ever have been failing to show up for their appointments at the scheduled time. One study, for example, indicated that seven million medical appointments were missed by patients in one year alone, a staggering figure with serious financial and health consequences. In what way might active commitments be harnessed to help alleviate the problem? When we make appointments for our next visit—whether it's for a routine checkup or important surgery—it's standard practice that the receptionist or administrator of the unit writes down the date and time of that next appointment on a little reminder card. With such a routine, however, the patient's role is passive rather than active. Asking patients to fill out the card themselves is not only more effective, but saves staff time as well.

Finally, as with many other approaches described in this book, active commitments can be useful to generate compliance in our personal lives, too. A small but psychologically significant action such as securing an active, written commitment from our children, neighbors, friends, partners, or even ourselves can often mean the difference between being able to influence others effectively versus soliciting commitments that others have all the intention in the world of fulfilling, but somehow never get around to.

18

How can you fight consistency with consistency?

According to Oscar Wilde, "Consistency is the last refuge of the unimaginative." A similarly disdainful Ralph Waldo Emerson said, "A foolish consistency is the hobgoblin of little minds." And finally, Aldous Huxley noted, "The only truly consistent people are dead." Why is it more likely that these famous authors made these statements when they were young whippersnappers rather than when they were elderly sages, and what could this mean for your attempts to influence others?

As we discussed earlier in the book, people generally prefer their behavior to be consistent with their preexisting attitudes, statements, values, and actions. But how does the aging process alter this inclination? Along with lead researcher Stephanie Brown and another colleague, one of us conducted a study showing that people's preference for consistency becomes greatly strengthened as they get older. This is likely the case because inconsistency can be emotionally upsetting, and older people have greater motivation to avoid emotionally upsetting experiences.[34]

This finding has important implications for how we try to influence older people. For example, suppose you work for a company that's attempting to market a range of new products to a more mature audience. Our research suggests that this particular demographic is going to be more resistant to change than others. In such a case, you'd be well advised to focus your messages on how purchasing and using the product is consistent with the audience's pre-existing values, beliefs, and practices. The same lesson can be applied in other domains, such as convincing an older member of a work team to switch to a new system, or even getting one's elderly parent to take his or her medication.

But do people really give up their previous behavior that easily—simply by being told that the new suggested behavior is consistent with their pre-existing practices, beliefs, and values? What about the original decisions they made to behave the way they do? From their point of view, remaining consistent with those decisions is probably a good thing. After all, everyone knows how frustrating it can be to deal with people who are routinely inconsistent, who constantly change their mind, who are easily influenced by the very next message they hear, who are indecisive.

Such a situation requires us to do something else in addition to pointing out how our proposal aligns with what they have previously declared to be important to them. To ensure our message is optimally persuasive, we need not only to free them from their previous commitment, but also to avoid framing their previous decision as a mistake. Perhaps the most productive method is to praise their previous decision as correct "*at the time that they made it.*" Pointing out that the previous choices they made were the right ones "*given the evidence and information they had at the time*" can help free them from such a commitment and allow them to focus on your proposal without the need for loss of face or inconsistency.

With this "prepersuasion" statement, your next message, still aligned to their overall values, beliefs, and practices, has legs. In the same way that a painter will prepare a canvas before painting, a medical professional will prepare surgical equipment before operating, and a sports coach will prepare her team before a match, a persuasive appeal requires preparation, too. And sometimes such preparation requires us not only to consider how to pitch our message but also to pay attention to previous messages that have been acted upon for many years. As the saying goes, the best way to ride a horse is in the *direction that the horse is going.* Only by first aligning to the direction the horse is going is it possible to then slowly and deliberately steer it where you'd like to go. Simply trying to pull the horse immediately in the desired direction will just wear you out—and you'll probably just upset the horse in the process.

19

What persuasion tip can you borrow from Benjamin Franklin?

Born in 1706, Benjamin Franklin is renowned as a leading author, politician, diplomat, scientist, publisher, philosopher, and inventor. As a politician, perhaps more than any other, he encouraged the very idea of an American nation. As a diplomat during the American Revolution, he secured the French alliance that helped to make independence possible. As a scientist, he was a major figure for his discoveries and theories regarding electricity. And as an inventor, he was responsible for the creation of bifocals, the odometer, and the lightning rod. But it's what he discovered about how to win over respect of his opposition—by inconveniencing them, no less—that might be most electrifying of all.[35]

When Franklin was in the Pennsylvania legislature, he was deeply bothered by the staunch political opposition and hostility of another legislator. Franklin himself best explains how he successfully won his respect and even his friendship:

I did not, however, aim at gaining his favor by paying any servile respect to him, but, after some time, took this other method. Having heard that he had in his library a certain very scarce and curious book, I wrote a note to him, expressing my desire of perusing that book, and requesting he would do me the favor of lending it to me for a few days. He sent it immediately, and I return'd it in about a week with another note, expressing strongly my sense of the favor. When we next met in the House, he spoke to me (which he had never done before), and with great civility; and he ever after manifested a readiness to serve me on all occasions, so that we became great friends, and our friendship continued to his death. This is another instance of the truth of an old maxim I had learned, which says, "He that has once done you a kindness will be more ready to do you another, than he whom you yourself have obliged."[36]

A century later, researchers Jon Jecker and David Landy set out to see if Franklin was right. In one study, participants won some money from the experimenter in a contest. Afterward, one group of participants was approached by the experimenter, who asked them if they'd be willing to give back the money because he was using his own money and had little left. (Almost all agreed.) Another group of participants was not approached with any request. All of the participants were then anonymously surveyed about how much they liked the experimenter.

Was Franklin's strategy, as illogical as it sounds, supported? Indeed it was. Jecker and Landy found that those who were asked to do the favor for the experimenter rated the experimenter more favorably than did those who were not asked to give back the money.[37]

Why? We know from other studies that people are strongly motivated to change their attitudes in ways that are consistent with their behavior. When Franklin's opponent found himself doing a favor for someone he didn't care for, he probably had to say to himself, "Why am I going out of my way to help out this person I don't even like? Perhaps Franklin's not so bad after all. Come to think of it, he does have some redeeming qualities . . ."

Franklin's strategy lends itself to managing relationships in any number of different environments. To take one, often we are in need of assistance from a coworker, colleague, or neighbor who, for one reason or another, doesn't view us in a particularly favorable light. We might be reluctant to ask for the favor because we're afraid this person will like us even less. Rather than ask for such a favor, a more typical tendency is to put off the request, potentially delaying a timely accomplishment of the task at hand. The results of this research indicate that such hesitation is unwarranted.

Now, in the case of some objectionable people, asking for a favor might seem to be a rather brave thing to do. But consider the following: If you currently have nothing to show from your communications (or noncommunications) with this person, the worst thing that will happen is that you'll end up with the same nothing. Try it. You truly have nothing to lose.

20

When can asking for a little go a long way?

Presumably a very little person first said, "Good things come in small packages." Whoever coined the phrase, it's clear that this person understood the power of thinking big by going small.

Throughout this book, we've attempted to provide evidence to support our claims that we can successfully and ethically move people to say yes. But in certain situations and environments, it's also important to understand why people say no to reasonable requests, such as a request to donate to a legitimate charity.

Along with several colleagues, one of us set out to do just that. We thought that when asked to make a donation, even those who would genuinely like to support the charity in some way say no because they can't afford to donate very much and they assume the small amount they can afford won't do much to help the cause. Based on this reasoning, we thought that one way to urge people in this situation to donate would be to inform them that even an extremely small sum would be helpful to the cause, essentially legitimizing such contributions.

To test this hypothesis, our research assistants went door-to-door to request donations for the American Cancer Society. After introducing themselves, these research assistants asked the residents, "Would you be willing to help by giving a donation?" For half of the residents, the request ended there. For the other half, however, the research assistant added, "Even a penny will help."

When we analyzed the results, we found that this diminutive disk of copper and zinc was worth its weight in persuasive gold. Consistent with our hypothesis, people in the "even-a-penny-will-help" condition were almost twice as likely as those in the other condition to donate to the cause (50 percent vs. 28.6 percent).[38]

On the face of it, the study suggests that when you want assistance from others, simply pointing out that even a small offering would be acceptable and worthwhile to you is likely to be an effective strategy. Still, is there a possibility that adopting an "even-a-penny-will-help" strategy could backfire? Although the number of people who donated almost doubled when people were told that even a penny would help, might their donations have been smaller than those in the other condition? After all, those residents were informed that even a single cent would help, which might have led them to give a smaller donation than they ordinarily would. We looked at the size in donation amounts and were happy to find that there was no difference in the average donation per contributor. What this means is that the "even-a-penny-will-help" request should come out ahead of a standard request not only in the number of people who donate, but in the overall amount collected from your efforts.

In our study, for instance, for every hundred people we asked, we collected seventy-two dollars in donations in the "even-a-penny" condition compared to only forty-four dollars in the standard condition.

There are several applications of the "even-a-penny-will-help" approach in the workplace. To coworkers regarding a community project, "Just an hour of your time would really help." To a colleague whose handwriting is illegible, "Just a little more clarity would help." To a busy prospective client whose needs must be more fully understood, "Even a brief initial phone call would help." The chances are that this little step in your direction won't prove so little after all.

21

Start low or start high? Which will make people buy?

What can items such as gum chewed by Britney Spears, a Papa Smurf commemorative plate, or a broken laser pointer teach us about how to most effectively sell goods and services through a competitive bidding process? For example, can an examination of how people list their "treasures" on eBay tell us whether we should use a low starting price or a high starting price?

eBay Inc. is the company that manages ebay.com, the online auction and shopping website where people and businesses buy and sell goods and services worldwide. It was founded in 1995 in San Jose, California, by a computer programmer named Pierre Omidyar, who ran a consulting company called the Echo Bay Technology Group. When he attempted to register his consultancy group's website, he found that echobay.com had already been taken by the gold-mining company Echo Bay Mines, so he shortened the company name and ebay.com was born. The very first item to appear on eBay was Omidyar's broken laser pointer, which he sold for $14.83. Astonished that someone would want to buy such an item, he contacted the winning bidder and asked if he understood that the laser pointer was broken. Responding to the email, the buyer explained: "I'm a collector of broken laser pointers."

In 2006, eBay registered some $6 billion in sales on a site where it is now possible to buy pretty much anything you can imagine—and sometimes beyond. In recent years, some of the more notable sales included the original Hollywood sign, an entire city in California, and the rights to choose a seller's new middle name. An Arizona man successfully managed to sell his prized air guitar for $5.50 even though he pointed out that bidders were in fact buying nothing, and in 2005 the clearly outraged wife of a U.K. radio disc jockey sold his beloved Lotus Esprit sports car for a "Buy It Now" price of fifty pence (about ninety cents at the time) after she heard him flirting on the airwaves with a glamour model. The car sold in five minutes.

Clearly ebay.com has identified a hugely successful business model, based on online auctions. Many companies have adopted similar models using online bidding processes and systems to secure tenders and choose vendors. Because of the inherent similarities between an online auction's bidding processes and a business's competitive bidding process, observing how sellers most effectively sell their stuff on websites like eBay can teach us quite a bit about how to most effectively manage a company's competitive bidding.

Behavioral scientist Gillian Ku and her colleagues knew that when the initial price for an item is high, as a potential buyer, you're likely to think it's worth more than if the initial price were lower. Yet, they wondered whether the increase in perceived value that comes along with a high starting price would actually lead to a higher final sale price. Instead, based on their research, they suggest that *lower* starting prices can actually lead to a higher final sale price, for three reasons.

First, because the starting prices for auctions act as somewhat of a barrier to entry, lower starting prices are better for encouraging participation by as many people as possible in the bidding process for an item. Second, the increase in traffic—reflected in the total number of bids as well as the number of different bidders—afforded by these lower initial prices acts as social proof for new potential bidders. In other words, prospective bidders considering an item that started off at a low price would find social validation that the item is of value because so many more people were also bidding on the item, and this validation would spur them to bid on the item as well. Third, bidders for items with low starting prices, especially those who get in early, are likely to spend more time and effort updating their bids. In an effort to justify the time and energy they've already spent on the bidding process, these bidders are more likely to stay committed to winning the auction by continuing to bid and raising their bids even higher.[39]

These research findings suggest that if you are in the business of offering goods or services through any kind of competitive bidding process, starting the bidding at a fairly low price can be a way of enhancing the final sale price. However, there is one very important caveat to consider: The researchers found that the social proof component was a critical factor in the enhanced effectiveness of the lower starting price. So, when the traffic for a particular item was constrained (for example, due to a misspelling of the product name, which limits the number of prospective bidders who are likely to find the item through a typical eBay search), the lower starting price was less effective. This means that a lower starting price is likely to be most effective when there's a possibility that many bidders will join the bidding fray for your product but is likely to be least effective when the bidding is limited to only two potential parties.

Although taking this advice might not earn you millions of extra dollars on your company's widgets or your family's antique thimble collection, at the very least it should help you earn enough to bid on that air guitar, should the original buyer decide to resell it.

22

How can we show off what we know
without being labeled a show-off?

If you're like most people, when you know best,
you want to tell the whole world about it. But even
when you have the credentials to present yourself as a
knowledgeable authority on a topic, there's a formidable
dilemma to overcome: In trying to convey your expertise to others, and in attempting to persuade them toward
your point of view, you might come across as boastful
and conceited. As a result, they may like you less, and
possibly even be less inclined to follow your advice. With
unabashed self-promotion out of the question, what's a
genuine expert to do?

One option is to get someone else to speak on your
behalf. This approach has been widely accepted by
speakers, authors, performers, and other public communicators for many years. Arranging for someone else to
introduce your expertise and credentials to your audience will do wonders to convince them that they should
listen to what you have to say, while also avoiding the
damage that blatant self-promotion can cause. Ideally,
this person would be a "true believer" in your skills and

knowledge and volunteer to tell everyone how smart you are in the hope that you'll make the world a better place. But your mother isn't always available. Instead, you can hire a representative to do the job.

But won't people completely discount the words of the representative, who is being paid to sing your praises? Not if they commit one of the most common errors that people make, which social psychologists call the fundamental attribution error: When observing another person's behavior, we tend not to give sufficient weight to the role situational factors (e.g., money) play in shaping that person's behavior.

In a set of studies one of us conducted with lead researcher Jeffrey Pfeffer and two other colleagues, we argued that people do not discount this information nearly as much as they should, which means that paying an intermediary to tout your abilities should still be an effective form of persuasion. In one of those studies, participants were asked to imagine themselves in the role of senior editor for a book publisher. In this role, they had the specific job of dealing with an experienced and successful author. They were asked to read excerpts from a negotiation for a sizable book advance. One group read excerpts touting the author's accomplishments spoken by the author's agent, whereas a second group read identical comments made by the author himself. The data verified our hypothesis: Participants rated the author more favorably on nearly every dimension—especially likability—when the author's agent sang his praises as compared to when the author tooted his own horn.[40]

This research confirms that having a skilled third party who will set up your initial presentation can be a very productive and worthwhile strategy for conveying your expertise in an area. In fact, where possible, that third party should also negotiate contract conditions and remuneration on your behalf. We'd also recommend that when giving a presentation to people who don't know you very well, you should arrange for someone else to introduce you to your audience. One of the most efficient ways of doing this is to ensure that you have prepared a short biography of yourself. This biography needn't be lengthy, but it should at the very least contain some information about your background, experience, training, or education that makes it clear that you are qualified to speak on a certain topic. You could also include several examples of successes that you've had on the topic on which you'll be speaking.

In fact, recently one of us had the opportunity to work with a real estate agency that used this approach to immediate and highly successful effect. The agency concerned has both a sales and a rental division. Consequently, customers who called into the office would typically first speak with a receptionist who, having identified which department they needed to speak with, would say, "Oh, rentals, you need to speak to Judy," or, "You need the sales department . . . let me put you through to Sheldon."

In response to our recommendation that her colleagues should be introduced along with their credentials, the receptionist now tells inquiring customers not only which of her colleagues they should speak to, but also her colleagues' expertise. As a result, customers who want further information about rentals are now told, "Oh, rentals, you need to speak to Judy, who has over fifteen years' experience renting properties in this neighborhood. Let me put you through now." Similarly, customers who want more information about selling their property are now told, "I'm going to put you through to Sheldon, our head of sales. Sheldon has twenty years of experience selling properties; in fact, he recently sold a property very similar to yours."

There are four notable features of this change. First, everything the receptionist tells her customers about her coworkers' experience is true. Judy does have fifteen years' experience, Sheldon is one of the most successful real estate salespeople. But for Sheldon or Judy to tell the customers themselves would be seen as boastful and self-promoting, and as a result, not nearly as persuasive. Second, it doesn't seem to matter that the introduction comes from someone who is clearly connected to Judy and Sheldon, who will both obviously benefit from such an introduction. The third notable feature is how effective it is. Judy, Sheldon, and their colleagues report a significant rise in the number of appointments they are generating compared to when they hadn't been introduced. And finally, it is important to note that the intervention was, for the most part, costless to implement. Everyone knew of the wide-ranging expertise and experience that resided in the office. Everyone, that is, except the most important people of all—the company's potential customers.

But what if it's impractical to have someone else sing your praises? Is there another subtle way of demonstrating that you are competent without saying so? Indeed there is. To take an example, one of us was approached by a group of physicians' assistants who were frustrated by their patients' noncompliance with important exercises that the patients needed to perform to get healthier. No matter how hard they tried to convey the necessity and urgency of doing these exercises, the patients would rarely follow their instructions. When we asked to see the examining room, one thing stuck out: There were no credentials whatsoever on the wall—or anywhere else, for that matter. After we advised them to put their credentials in places that their patients could see, the physicians' assistants reported a huge difference in patient compliance. The lesson? Display your diplomas, certificates, and awards to those you want to persuade. You've earned those credentials, and, in turn, they'll help you earn your audience's trust.

23

What's the hidden danger of being
the brightest person in the room?

O ver drinks, bar patrons have been known to tell
some dubious stories:

"I dated that supermodel before she got famous."

"I could've won the fight, but I didn't want to hurt the
other guy."

"I was accepted with a full scholarship to study at
MIT, but took a job sweeping floors there instead."

But on a cold and unpleasant February evening in
1953, two gentlemen walked into the Eagle Public House
in Cambridge, England, and after ordering their drinks,
one of them publicly announced to the other patrons
what must have seemed like the tallest tale of all: "We
have found the secret of life."

Although their claim might seem rather boastful and
arrogant, it was nonetheless true. That morning, scientists James Watson and Francis Crick had indeed found
the secret of life: They had discovered the double-helix
structure of DNA, the biological material that carries
life's genetic information.

On the fiftieth anniversary of what could be described

as perhaps the most important scientific discovery of our
time, Watson took part in an interview on the topic of this
accomplishment. The interview was designed to inquire
about the aspects of Watson and Crick's work that had
led them to solve the problem of the structure of DNA
ahead of an array of other highly accomplished and rec-
ognized rival scientists.

At first, Watson listed a set of contributory factors that
were largely unsurprising: It was crucial that he and Crick
had identified the problem that was the most important to
attack. They were both passionate about their work; they
devoted themselves single-mindedly to the task at hand.
They were willing to embrace and attempt approaches
that were outside their area of familiarity. But then he
added another reason for their success that was nothing
short of stunning. He and Crick had cracked the elusive
code for DNA primarily, he said, because they were *not*
the most intelligent scientists pursuing the answer.

Watson went on to explain that the most intelligent
person working on the project in those days was Rosa-
lind Franklin, a British scientist who was working in Paris
at the time.

> Rosalind was so intelligent that she rarely sought
> advice. And if you're the brightest person in the room,
> then you're in trouble.

Watson's comment shines light on a familiar error
seen in the actions of many well-intentioned leaders.
Leaders in organizations who are dealing with a specific
issue or problem—for example, how to design the most

effective sales pitch for a possible client, or how to create the most effective campaign to raise funds for a local parent-teacher association—should ensure that they collaborate with team members toward its resolution, even if they are the best-informed, most-experienced, or most-skilled person in the group. Not to do so would be foolhardy. In fact, behavioral scientist Patrick Laughlin and his colleagues have shown that the approaches and outcomes of groups who cooperate in seeking a solution are not just better than the average member working alone, but are even better than the group's best problem solver working alone. Far too often, leaders—who, by virtue of greater experience, skill, and wisdom, deem themselves the ablest problem solver in the group—fail to ask for input from team members.[41]

The research conducted by Laughlin and his colleagues tells us why the best leader operating individually will be beaten to a correct solution by an all-inclusive cooperating unit. First, lone decision-makers can't match the diversity of knowledge and perspectives of a multi-person unit that includes them. The input from others can stimulate thinking processes that wouldn't have been developed when working alone. We can all recall being led to an insight by the comment of a colleague who didn't deliver the insight but who sparked the association to the best solution. Second, the solution seeker who goes it alone loses another significant advantage—the power of parallel processing. Whereas a cooperating unit can distribute many subtasks of a problem to its members, a lone operator must perform each task sequentially.

But isn't full collaboration risky? After all, decisions

made completely by committee are notorious for sub-optimal performance. Mindful of that problem, our recommendation is not to employ a vote-counting strategy in order to come to a resolution; in fact the recommendation is not for making joint decisions at all. The final choice is always for the leader to make. But it's the process of seeking input that leaders should engage in more collectively. Those who arrange for regular team input can expect to achieve better outcomes. In addition, they can expect better relationships and rapport with their team, which enhances future collaboration and influence. But is there not a risk of bruised egos and lost motivation if a team member's idea is ultimately rejected? As long as a leader assures the team that each view—while perhaps not the deciding factor—will be considered in the process, this shouldn't occur. And who knows, although building a team of people who are encouraged and persuaded to offer insights, cooperate, and collaborate with each other may not enable you to declare, like Watson and Crick, that you "have found the secret to life," it may well help you to find the secret to unlocking your and your group's true potential.

24

Who is the better persuader? Devil's advocate or true dissenter?

In outer space exploration, two days of national mourning have been etched into history forever: On January 28, 1986, the U.S. shuttle *Challenger* exploded during liftoff. And on February 1, 2003, the U.S. shuttle *Columbia* was destroyed upon re-entry into Earth's atmosphere. Both disasters killed all seven crewmembers. Although the causes of the tragedies—in one case, damage to the leading edge of the shuttle's left wing, and in the other case, a failed O-ring seal on the shuttle's solid rocket booster—were different, a close examination of these failures suggests the same root cause: NASA's poor decision-making culture.

To understand how these disasters came about, consider the following exchange between a *Columbia* disaster investigator and the chairwoman of the mission management team:

Investigator: As a manager, how do you seek out dissenting opinions?

Chairwoman: Well, when I hear about them . . .

Investigator: By their very nature, you may not have
heard about them . . . what techniques do you
use to get them?[42]

The chairwoman had no answer.

The nature of these tragedies reminds us that sometimes
the goal should not be to persuade, but to *allow ourselves
to be persuaded by others* if we're leaning in the wrong direction. But how do we most effectively seek out dissenting
opinions? As leaders, can we simply ask a member of our
team to play devil's advocate?

For nearly four centuries, the Roman Catholic Church
relied on the Advocatus Diaboli, or devil's advocate, to
investigate and to present to the Church all the negative
aspects of the life and work of a candidate for sainthood.
In what might be referred to as a form of saintly due dili-
gence, the idea was that if there were a thorough investigation that uncovered all the unfavorable information
concerning the candidate and presented it to the Church
leadership, the decision-making process would be more
informed and would profit considerably from the diversity of ideas, perspectives, and sources of information.

Anyone who works in the business world knows that
the terms "business" and "sainthood" are not commonly
associated with each other. Yet business managers could
learn a valuable lesson from the devil's advocate procedure. When it seems that everyone on a team initially
agrees on an issue—be it a revamped business plan, a new
marketing strategy, or some other important topic—it can

often be fruitful to encourage and to seek out alternative points of view. This becomes even more important considering the potentially devastating effects of groupthink and group polarization, in which the majority opinion in a group becomes more extreme the more it is discussed.

Social psychologists have also known for some time that even one lone dissenter in an otherwise unanimous group may be enough to generate more creative and complex thinking within that group. But until recently, very little research had been conducted regarding the nature of the dissenter. Are devil's advocates—that is, pseudodissenters—better or worse than authentic dissenters at enhancing the problem-solving abilities of a group of otherwise like-minded people?

The results of a study conducted by social psychologist Charlan Nemeth and colleagues suggest that, in comparison to an authentic dissenter, a person asked to play the role of devil's advocate will be much less effective at promoting creative problem-solving among group members. The researchers argue that majority members are more likely to perceive the true dissenter's arguments and positions as principled and, therefore, as valid. The position favored by the devil's advocate, on the other hand, seems like disagreement simply for the sake of disagreement. When the majority members are confronted by a person who truly appears to oppose their position, they search to understand why the dissenter is so committed to his or her beliefs. In the process, they come to a better understanding of the problem and consider it from a broader perspective.[43]

Do these findings imply that the devil's advocate is outdated and obsolete? In the 1980s, Pope John Paul II officially eliminated the practice from the Church's storied process. Indeed, there's some evidence that experience with a devil's advocate has the potential to *strengthen,* rather than weaken, majority members' confidence in their original position, presumably because they believe that they have considered—and subsequently dismissed—all possible alternatives.[44]

Considering the findings of this research, perhaps the best policy for leaders is to create and sustain a work environment in which coworkers and subordinates not only feel welcome but are also encouraged to openly disagree with the majority viewpoint. This could well translate into more innovative solutions to complex problems and greater overall employee morale (as long as dissension remains professional and not personal), and could eventually lead to increased profits. In situations in which decisions will have long-lasting and potentially far-reaching implications, consideration should also be given to actually seeking out true dissenters. By encouraging knowledgeable others to passionately persuade us that we may be leaning in the wrong direction, we place ourselves in a position to gain a greater understanding from a genuine argument rather than a simulated one, allowing us to make optimal decisions and create maximally effective messages.

Unfortunately, there are all too many counterexamples of this orientation, where higher-ranked and more-experienced leaders create an atmosphere in which subordinates are afraid to question the leaders' decisions. Even in situations in which the subordinates are correct, it's too often the case that employees are reluctant to disagree with their managers, nurses are hesitant to question their supervising doctors, and first officers defer to their aircraft's captains. For leaders to create a better environment, the first step is to have a little humility. In other words, just remember to check your ego at the boardroom, hospital, or cockpit door.

25

When can the right way be
the wrong way?

Strength. Courage. Determination. Commitment. Selflessness. Some might say that our firefighters should be role models for how we behave both within and outside our organizations. Even though saving lives and rescuing kittens from trees might not be in your work description, learning how firefighters train for their job might just help you become an everyday hero in yours.

Behavioral researcher Wendy Joung and her colleagues were interested in examining whether certain types of training programs would be more effective than others at minimizing errors in judgment on the job. Specifically, they wanted to know whether focusing the trainee on past errors that others have made would provide better training than focusing the trainee on how others had made good decisions in the past. They thought that training that focused more on others' errors would be more effective for several reasons, including increased attention to the training and a more memorable training experience.

Yes!

The researchers aimed to test their hypothesis on a group of people whose decision-making skills under stress were vital, and whose decisions carried important consequences; it's not surprising that they chose firefighters. In the study, a training and development session that included several case studies was presented to the firefighters. However, the nature of the case studies differed between two groups of participants. One group learned from case studies that described real-life situations in which other firefighters made poor decisions that led to negative consequences. The other group learned from case studies in which firefighters avoided negative consequences through good decision-making. Joung and her colleagues found that firefighters who underwent the error-based training showed improved judgment and were able to think more adaptively than those who underwent the error-free training.[45]

Training is all about influencing others, so if you want to maximize your influence on employees' future behavior, the implications for your organization's training programs are clear. Although many companies typically focus their training exclusively on the positive—in other words, on how to make good decisions—the results of this study suggest that a sizable portion of the training should be devoted to how others have made errors in the past and how those errors could have been (and can be) avoided. Specifically, case studies, videos, illustrations, and personal testimonials of mistakes should be followed by a discussion of what actions would have been appropriate to take in these and similar situations.

Of course, specific individuals don't have to be singled out by management for their previous poor decision-making; these error-based experiences can be completely anonymous. However, you might find that some of the more experienced and respected employees are more than happy to donate their error-laden "war stories" to the company's training archive.

This approach shouldn't be limited to the corporate classroom. Teachers, tutors, sports coaches, and just about anyone who provides training to others can benefit from such an orientation. That includes parents, of course. For example, when teaching children to stay away from strangers, parents can describe hypothetical scenarios in which a child is tricked by a stranger. By focusing on what the child in the example could have done to get away from the stranger in that specific situation, parents will prepare their children to deal with such scenarios in the future.

26

What's the best way to turn a weakness into a strength?

Suppose that one day, you decide that you want to own two more copies of this book, for a total of three—one for home, one for the office, and one for the glove compartment of your car in case of emergencies. After you grab the last two copies of *Yes!* off the shelf at a local bookstore and bring them to the checkout counter, you are taken aback by something the clerk says. "Are you sure you want to buy those books here?" he asks. "I know we have one of the more competitive prices on that book, but the bookstore just down the street is selling it for about 15 percent less than our price. If you'd like, I can draw you a map of how to get there." With customer service like that—or more accurately, with *non*customer service like that—you wonder how this place is still standing.

Although this example may sound somewhat absurd, some businesses have actually adopted this seemingly self-exterminating practice. For instance, take Progressive Auto Insurance, the third-largest auto insurance company in the United States. The company has always prided itself on innovations that distinguish it from its competitors, including being the first major insurance company in the world to launch a website, in 1995. One year later, car owners searching for auto insurance rates could use the Progressive website not only to learn about Progressive's rates, but also to learn about the rates offered by Progressive's major competitors. Today, the company even features a "rate ticker" prominently on its homepage, which displays a scrolling information bar listing the various comparisons that recent visitors learned about. Although Progressive clearly has the better rates in many of these instances, this is certainly not always the case. For example, as we write this, within one minute of visiting the site, the rate ticker revealed that someone with the initials C.M. in Wisconsin would save almost $942 per year on insurance for his or her Toyota by choosing a competitor over Progressive.

So, is Progressive insuring more customers with this strategy, or is it ensuring its own extinction? The company's enormous growth since it implemented this innovation—an average of 17 percent a year, with annual premiums growing from $3.4 billion to $14 billion—suggests that it's quite effective at turning potential customers from "web browsers" into web buyers. Indeed, research conducted by social scientists Valerie Trifts and Gerald Häubl also supports Progressive's practices: Participants looking to buy books in a simulated online environment reported being more likely to shop from a moderately priced bookseller when that bookseller also provided its competitors' (sometimes lower) prices.[46]

To understand why this strategy is so successful, consider another example. Nearly half a century ago, the advertising firm of Doyle, Dane, & Bernbach was challenged with the almost insurmountable task of introducing a tiny German automobile to a U.S. market in which only larger domestic cars had previously thrived. Within a short period, the Volkswagen Beetle was transformed from a relatively obscure laughingstock to an extremely popular status symbol. The success of the Beetle can be largely attributed to the firm's engineering of one of the greatest ad campaigns in the history of advertising. This campaign certainly broke with the industry's conventional wisdom at the time: When promoting the brand, they didn't emphasize the product's strengths, such as the fact that it was relatively inexpensive or that it got good gas mileage. So what did they focus on, then?

They touted its weaknesses. These ads focused on the fact that the Volkswagen was not nearly as pleasing to the eye as the typical American-made cars of the day. For example, "Ugly is only skin deep" and "It will stay uglier longer" were some of the slogans used in the campaign. It's easy to understand why these headlines attracted attention, and it's easy to see why the campaign in general was very likable. But these factors alone can't account for the huge surge in sales that accompanied the launch and continuation of this campaign. Why do the types of marketing strategies employed by Progressive and Volkswagen succeed?

Arguing against your self-interest, which can include mentioning a drawback of your arguments, proposals, or products, creates the perception that you and your organization are honest and trustworthy. This puts you in a position to be more persuasive when promoting your genuine strengths. In Progressive's case, the company's strength is that many of its rates are truly superior to its competitors'. And in the case of Volkswagen, sure, the Beetle wouldn't win any beauty contests, but its strengths were durability, fuel economy, and price. Similarly, Avis car rental, the world's *second*-largest car rental company, took advantage of this principle in its memorable motto: "Avis. We're #2, but we try harder. (When you're not #1, you have to.)" Other examples include "The Peace Corps: The toughest job you'll ever love," "Motel 6: Our rooms aren't fancy, but our prices aren't fancy," "Listerine: The taste you hate three times a day," and "L'Oreal: We're more expensive, but you're worth it."

Evidence for this strategy has been found outside the domains of marketing as well. Consider one example of its use in law: Social psychologist Kip Williams and colleagues found that when jurors heard a lawyer mention a weakness in his own case before the opposing attorney mentioned it, jurors evaluated him as more trustworthy and were more favorable to his overall case in their verdicts because of that perceived honesty. In a second study, the same held true for an expert witness testifying for the prosecution in a civil trial: When the prosecution's witness volunteered the weakness in his testimony and then explained why the weakness wasn't especially important, verdicts were more likely to be in favor of the plaintiff (65 percent) than when the defense attorney was the one to first bring up the issue (43 percent).[47]

There are a number of other applications for this persuasion technique as well. For example, if you're selling your car, when a prospective buyer comes to give it a test drive, volunteering negative information about the car, especially information that the prospect would be unlikely to discover on his or her own (for example, that the light inside the trunk is a little touchy or the fuel economy is modest) should do wonders for his or her trust in you and your vehicle.

The strategy can also be applied at the negotiating table. For example, if there's a small area in which your leverage is weak, your negotiating partner is likely to see you as more trustworthy if you mention it up front rather than having it be discovered later. The same goes for direct sales: If you are selling color copiers to a business, and your copier holds slightly less paper than your competitors', it might be helpful to mention that fact early on in the process to earn the potential buyer's trust. Then, it will be easier to convince the buyer that the truly superior features of your copier really do surpass the competition in those areas.

Note, however, that you're going to be able to use this strategy effectively only if your weaknesses are genuinely minor ones. This is why we rarely see ad campaigns with mottos like, "Ranked last in its class by J. D. Power and Associates, but once we get these wrongful death suits taken care of, we'll try harder."

27

Which faults unlock people's vaults?

François, Duc de La Rochefoucauld, the seventeenth-century French writer and moralist, foreshadowed the astonishing success of the famed Volkswagen Beetle advertising campaign when he wrote, "We only confess our little faults to persuade people that we have no big ones." Although that campaign seemed to handle its product's faults deftly, attempting to use such messages leaves us with a dilemma: *Which* little faults should we choose to confess?

Research conducted by social scientist Gerd Bohner and his colleagues suggests that for such "two-sided" persuasive appeals to be maximally effective, there must be a clear connection between the negative and positive attributes that are conveyed. In one study, Bohner created three different versions of an advertisement for a restaurant. One message featured only positive product attributes of the restaurant. To take just one example, the advertisement touted the restaurant's cozy atmosphere. A second message mentioned those positive features in addition to some unrelated negative ones. For example, in addition to mentioning the cozy atmosphere, the advertisement stated that the restaurant couldn't offer dedicated parking to its clients. The third message described certain negative features and added some related positive ones. In this message, for instance, the ad described the restaurant as very small, but it also mentioned that it had a cozy atmosphere.

So, participants who saw the third advertisement were able to make the connection between the negative aspects of the restaurant and the positive ones ("There's little space, but that's part of what makes the atmosphere cozy"). In short, although both types of two-sided messages produced increases in the restaurant owner's perceived credibility, the evaluation of the restaurant itself was highest in the two-sided message in which the positive and negative attributes were related.[48]

These findings indicate that if you're primarily looking to increase your trustworthiness in the eyes of others, the particular types of weaknesses you convey in your two-sided messages are less likely to matter. However, if you're also looking to enhance their positive feelings specifically toward the object of discussion—be it a restaurant, a product, or even your credentials—then you'd be well advised to ensure that any dark cloud you describe is paired with a silver lining tailored to that particular cloud. To take a real-life example, when U.S. president Ronald Reagan was up for re-election in 1984, some voters were concerned that he was too old to have an effective second term in office. During the U.S. presidential debate against opponent Walter Mondale, Reagan acknowledged that he was very old, but stated: "I want you to know that also I will not make age an issue of this campaign. I am not going to exploit for political purposes my opponent's youth and inexperience." Although Mondale's immediate response was to let out a laugh, he was certainly not laughing when he was later routed in one of the biggest landslide losses in U.S. presidential history.

This research has many business applications, as well. For instance, let's say that you're presenting a product that your company has recently launched to a new client. It has some notable features and benefits over that of your competitors, but these features and benefits come at a cost. As a result, it carries a price premium some 20 percent more than the product that this new client company is currently using. However, you also have information that this initial 20 percent premium is offset by the fact that your product lasts longer and is more cost effective to maintain. It's also faster and more compact, using up significantly less space than your competitor's.

The results of this research suggest that after you mention the weakness of the price premium, you should follow that statement with a benefit related to cost and not any other attribute of your product. Therefore, a statement such as, "On the face of it, our new product has a 20 percent price premium, but this is more than offset when you consider how much longer it lasts and the lower maintenance costs," would be more persuasive than the statement that "On the face of it, our new product has a 20 percent price premium, but it's much faster and also takes up less space."

Yes!

In other words, be sure to follow your discussion of a drawback with a positive aspect that's related to, and that neutralizes, the drawback. In other words, when fate gives us lemons, we should try to make lemonade, not apple juice.[49]

28

When is it right to admit that you were wrong?

In February 2007, JetBlue Airways, the New York-based, low-cost American airline, frustrated thousands of passengers due to a lack of preparation and poor decision-making in the face of severe winter weather in the northeastern United States. Almost without exception, all other airlines that provided passenger service in that region had canceled massive numbers of flights in anticipation of the storm. They then returned to normal service within a couple of days. In contrast, JetBlue gave hope to many of its passengers that their planes would fly—yet they remained out of service for many days. In short, the storms never let up, so many of JetBlue's customers were let down.

After stranding thousands of passengers in airports and on tarmacs in this operational nightmare, JetBlue had a difficult public relations decision to make: who or what to blame? Should they focus the blame on external factors, like the extreme weather, or should they focus the blame on internal factors relevant to the company's operations at large? The company chose the latter, acknowl-

119

edging JetBlue's failures during the meltdown were caused by internal rather than external problems. It takes bravery and a sense of humility to admit one's mistakes, which is perhaps why it is so rare to see organizations and the people within them take the blame for a misstep or a misjudgment. Does the social influence research support the decision by JetBlue to do what many companies in its position would probably never even consider?

Social scientist Fiona Lee and her colleagues suggest that organizations that attribute failures to internal causes will come out ahead not only in public perception, but also in terms of the profit line. They argue that blaming internal, potentially controllable failures makes the organization appear to have greater control over its own resources and future. They also suggest that the public response to an organization's internal focus to explain failures might be to assume that the organization has a plan to modify the internal features of the organization that may have led to the problems in the first place.

To test these ideas, Lee and colleagues conducted a brief study in which participants read one of two annual reports of a fictitious company, both of which explained why the company had performed so poorly over the last year. For half of the participants, the annual report blamed internal (but potentially controllable) factors for the poor performance:

Fictitious Company Report A

The unexpected drop in earnings this year is primarily attributable to some of the strategic decisions we made last year. Decisions to acquire a new company and to push out several new drugs in international markets directly contributed to short-term decreases in earnings. As a management team, we were not fully prepared for the unfavorable conditions that emerged from both the domestic and international sectors.

For the other half of the participants, the annual report blamed external (and uncontrollable) factors for the poor performance:

Fictitious Company Report B

The drop in earnings this year is primarily attributable to the unexpected downturn in the domestic and international economic environment and increased international competition. These unfavorable market conditions directly contributed to a short-term slump in sales and difficulties in the introduction of several key drugs to the market. These unexpected conditions arose from federal legislations and are completely outside our control.

Participants in the first condition (Report A) viewed the company more positively on a number of different dimensions than did participants in the second condition (Report B).

But the researchers didn't stop there—they wanted to test their hypothesis in a natural setting. To do this, they collected hundreds of these types of statements from the annual reports of fourteen companies over a twenty-one-year period. They discovered that when these companies explained failures in their annual reports, those that pointed to internal and controllable factors had higher stock prices one year later than those that pointed to external and uncontrollable factors.[50]

So, if taking responsibility for your mistakes and admitting that you're wrong is not only the right thing to do but also right for your company, why is this behavior such a rarity? Often the usual response to a costly or embarrassing error, regardless of whether it is an organization or an individual making the mistake, is to attempt to blame someone or some external factors to divert attention from the source of the problem. By taking such an approach, we create two bigger problems for ourselves. First, as the research suggests, this strategy is likely to be ineffective because it does nothing to prove to skeptics that we have any control over the problem or that we have the ability to fix the problem. Second, even if we do manage to distract attention from our mistake in the short term, the spotlight—or perhaps more accurately, the bull's-eye—will eventually find its way back to us in the long term, potentially highlighting not only our mistake but also our deceptive impulses.

This should hold true not only for companies, but for individuals, too. If you've made a mistake, an error in judgment, or a bad decision, you should admit the mistake, immediately followed by an action plan demonstrating that you can take control of the situation and rectify it. Through these actions, you'll ultimately put yourself in a position of greater influence by being perceived as not only capable, but also honest.

In sum, the results of this research suggest that if you play the blame game—pointing your finger at external factors rather than at yourself—both you and your organization will likely end up as the losers.

29

How can similarities make a difference?

In the summer of 1993, the floodwaters of the Mississippi River threatened to devastate several cities in the Midwest, including the city of Quincy, Illinois. In response to the imminent danger, Quincy residents worked night and day to secure vulnerable areas with thousands of sandbags. Things looked bleak for the residents; supplies and food were on the decline while fatigue, pessimism, and water levels were on the rise. The mood among the volunteers brightened considerably, however, when they learned that residents of a small city in Massachusetts had donated a large amount of provisions that was already en route to their location.

What was it that influenced the people of a seemingly random city to act so generously toward a town located a thousand miles away? And why help Quincy in particular, out of all the many cities and towns threatened by floodwaters?

A substantial amount of psychological research has shown that we're most likely to relate to others with whom we share personal characteristics, such as values, beliefs, age, and sex. But the reason behind this town's behavior lies in a subtle and seemingly irrelevant similarity between the two municipalities—they have the same name. Based simply on a shared name, the residents of Quincy, Massachusetts, felt a bond with the people of Quincy, Illinois, one that was strong enough to motivate their generosity.

How can this be explained? Social psychologists have found that we tend to feel especially positive toward subtle things that we associate with ourselves, such as our names. This tendency has manifested itself in some surprisingly powerful ways. Evidence suggests, for example, that people are more likely to comply with a stranger's request when the two share the same birthday.

In one set of studies, researcher Randy Garner sent surveys by mail to perfect strangers. Accompanying the survey was a request to complete and return it made by a person whose name was either similar or dissimilar to the name of the survey recipient. For example, in the similar-name condition, a person whose name was Robert Greer might get the survey from someone named Bob Gregar or a woman named Cynthia Johnston might get the survey from someone named Cindy Johanson. The names used in the not-similar condition were one of five names of the real research assistants involved in the study. Those who received the survey from someone with a similar-sounding name were nearly twice as likely to fill out and return the packet than were those who received the surveys from names that were not similar (56 percent compared to 30 percent). In fact, after the first phase of the study was completed, all who had returned the original survey were sent another survey assessing what role various factors might have played in their decision to return the packet. For this survey, roughly half responded, but none of the participants indicated that the name of the sender affected their decision to complete the packet. Findings such as these show both the power and the subtlety of similarity as a cue that people use to decide whom to help.[51]

Potential clients may thus be more receptive to a sales pitch from a salesperson with whom they share similarities in any number of domains, including names, beliefs, hometowns, and alma maters. Pointing out similarities can also be the first step to resolving potentially ugly conflicts with coworkers and even neighbors. Of course, we're not advocating that people invent similar characteristics or attributes with others to gain their favor. But what we are suggesting is that if you do share genuine similarities with someone, you should bring those similarities to the surface in your discussions with that person before making your request or presentation.

30

When is your name your game?

In one episode of the hit NBC comedy *The Office,* branch manager Michael Scott discovers that his sycophantic underling, Dwight Schrute, has gone behind his back to try to convince upper management to award Michael's job to him. To cover up his absence at work, Dwight tells Michael that he needs to go to the dentist to have a crown put in. When Dwight returns to the office, Michael asks him about his experience at the dentist, including a question about why Dwight is munching on candy when he just supposedly had major dental work. Unaware that Michael has learned about the coup attempt, Dwight tries to bluff. He tells Michael that the dentist gave him a new type of quick-drying bonding. Pretending to be impressed, Michael asks him his dentist's name, and after a long, awkward pause, Dwight replies, "Crentist."

Michael: Your dentist's name is Crentist?
Dwight: Yeah.
Michael: Huh . . . sounds a lot like dentist.
Dwight: Maybe that's why he became a dentist.[52]

Although Dwight's explanation of how "Dr. Crentist" became attracted to the profession of dentistry sounds ridiculous—even idiotic—new research makes it clear that claims like Dwight's might actually have a basis in reality. In the previous chapter, we discussed how people tend to have more positive feelings toward—and are more likely to comply with requests from—others who are similar to themselves in some way, even in superficial ways like sharing similar-sounding names. But is it possible that our names can affect important, life-altering decisions, such as the type of career we decide to pursue or where we decide to live?

Research conducted by social psychologist Brett Pelham and his colleagues suggests that the answer is yes. They claim that the tendency to favor things we associate with our names does in fact have a subtle but powerful influence on major life decisions, such as the career path we choose to follow. According to the researchers, there's a reason Susie chose a job in which she could sell seashells by the seashore and why Peter Piper picked a profession picking pecks of pickled peppers, not the other way around: People are attracted to professions with names similar to their own.

To test this idea, Pelham came up with a list of names that sounded like the word 'dentist,' such as Dennis. According to census data, the name Dennis was the fortieth-most-frequent male first name in the U.S. population at the time, with the names Jerry and Walter ranking thirty-ninth and forty-first, respectively. Armed with this information, Pelham searched the national directory of the American Dental Association, examining the number of dentists with one of those three first names. If people's names have no effect whatsoever on what career path they follow, you'd expect there to be roughly equal numbers of people with these three names going into the field of dentistry.[53]

But that's not what Pelham and his colleagues found. The nationwide search revealed that 257 dentists were named Walter, 270 were named Jerry, and 482 were named Dennis. That means that dentists are about 43 percent more likely to be named Dennis than you'd expect if name similarity had absolutely no effect on career choice. Similarly, people whose names begin with "Geo" (e.g., George, Geoffrey) are disproportionately likely to do research in the geosciences (e.g., geology). In fact, even just the first letter of a person's name influences his or her career choice. For example, they found that hardware store owners are around 80 percent more likely to have names that start with the letter "H" than the letter "R," but roofers are about 70 percent more likely to have names that start with the letter "R" than the letter "H." Of course, if you were to ask, say, a thousand roofers whose names begin with "R" whether their names played any role at all in the career they chose, it's likely that half of them would look at you as if you were crazy and the other half would look at you as if you were just stupid.*

---

*This fact was highlighted at a recent conference where one of us was speaking. Keen to point out a situation where there was no similarity between a person's name and career, a participant commented, "I have a friend named Dennis and he's not a dentist." When asked by another participant what Dennis did in fact do for

Yes!

It turns out that the tendency to be drawn to things that are associated with ourselves plays out in other important areas of life, including where we decide to live. To mention just a few of their findings, Pelham and his colleagues have shown that, at a disproportionate rate:

- People move to states that are similar to their own names. For example, people who move to Florida are disproportionately likely to be named Florence, and people who move to Louisiana are disproportionately likely to be named Louise.

- People move to cities with numbers in them that match their own birthdate numbers. For example, cities with the number 2 in their names, like Two Harbors, Minnesota, have a disproportionate number of residents who were born on February 2 (2/2), whereas cities that have the number 3 in their names, like Three Forks, Montana, have a disproportionate number of people who were born on March 3 (3/3).

- People choose to live on streets whose names match their own. In other words, someone named Mr. Washington is more likely to choose to live on Washington Street than someone named Mr. Jefferson.

---

a living, he let out a huge sigh and said, "Actually, he's a demolition worker."

- People choose to marry others who have similar-sounding first or last names. All else being roughly equal, if Eric, Erica, Charles, and Charlotte all meet one another for the first time, Erica will be more likely to become romantically involved with Eric than with Charles, and the opposite is more likely to occur with Charlotte.[54]

- When asked to trust their feelings and intuitions, people prefer products whose first letters matched the first letters of their own name. So, someone named Allan might be more likely to put the candy bar Almond Joy toward the top of his list than someone named Nick, who might be more likely to put Nutrageous toward the top of his list.[55]

This research suggests that if you're designing a program, initiative, or product that's being tailored for a specific client, you can harness the power of people's natural tendency to be attracted to things that remind them of themselves in the name, title, or label that you give it. Specifically, you should name it based on the client's name or even just the first letter of the client's name. For example, if you're considering pitching a strategy to someone named Peterson at Pepsi, calling the strategy the Pepsi Proposal or even something like the Peterson Plan would likely be effective. And, as long as the program is truly customized for a particular client, the strategy should not only be successful but also completely costless.

Similarly, if you're having difficulty getting your child interested in reading books, finding one that shares some name commonality with him or her (Harold or Harriet could be offered Harry Potter) might just be the key to getting him or her excited about it. Or, if little Craig or Crystal is deathly afraid of paying a visit to the dentist, you could always look in the Yellow Pages to see if you can find one named Crentist . . .

31

What tips should we take from
those who get them?

From business lunches with clients to bonding
experiences with our colleagues, friends, and
family, restaurants play a vital role in the success of both
our professional and personal lives. Although there's
quite a bit to be gained by interacting with our dining
partners in such a setting, the next great tip you get from
a restaurant visit might just come from a different group
of people—a group that hopes to get great tips all day, but
is seldom asked to dish any out.

Waiters can teach us a great deal about how to be
more persuasive. To take one example, many food servers have found that they receive larger tips when they
repeat their customers' orders back to them exactly as the
customer verbalized it. Many of us have had the experience of a waiter or waitress taking our order and then
passively saying "okay," or worse still, not even acknowl-
edging our order. No surprise, then, that we're left sitting at the table wondering whether the cheeseburger we
ordered will arrive at our table reincarnated as a chicken
sandwich.

Some research by Rick van Baaren tested the idea that food servers who match their customers' verbalizations after receiving the order will increase their tip size. No paraphrasing, no nodding, no "okays"—just repeating back word for word the customer's order. In one study, they found that the food servers at one restaurant increased their tip size by nearly 70 percent simply by matching their customers' verbalizations after receiving the order, as opposed to saying "okay!" or "coming up!"[56]

Why should mirroring another person elicit such a generous response from that person? Perhaps it ties into our natural inclination to prefer people who are similar to us. In fact, social psychologists Tanya Chartrand and John Bargh argue that matching the behavior of others creates feelings of liking and strengthens bonds between two people. In one experiment, the researchers set up a situation in which a research assistant either mirrored the posture and behavior of a subject—for example, if the participant sat cross-armed and tapped her foot, the research assistant sat cross-armed and tapped her foot—or did not.

The researchers found that the participants who had been mirrored liked the research assistant more and felt that the interaction was smoother than did participants whose behavior had not been mirrored. Similarly, food servers who match their customers' verbalizations probably garnered more tips because of the liking principle—that we want to do nice things for and say "yes" to people we like.[57]

Recently, researcher William Maddux and his colleagues conducted a set of experiments examining these processes in a different domain: negotiation. They suggested that behavior mirroring during negotiations could produce better outcomes not only for the person matching the other's behavior, but for both parties. For example, in one experiment, MBA students were either instructed to subtly mirror their partner (e.g., lean back in your chair if the other person does) during a negotiation or were not asked to mirror that person. When one party was instructed to mirror the other, the two parties reached a deal 67 percent of the time. When they weren't told to mirror the other? Only a paltry 12.5 percent. Based on some additional data from the experiment, the researchers concluded that behavior-mirroring led to increased trust, and that increased trust typically led one negotiator to feel comfortable disclosing details that were ultimately necessary to break a stalemate and create a win-win situation for both parties.[58]

We've all had experiences when we're in a meeting with a team member or we're negotiating with an adversary, and we notice that our postures are mirroring theirs. A typical response to this realization is to change our physical positioning and posturing so that it no longer mirrors the other person's—in other words, we act as if there were something wrong with behavior-matching. This research suggests the exact opposite: The mirroring should result in *better* outcomes for you both, or at the very least, the benefit to you won't come at the expense of the other person.

There are other applications of these findings as well. For example, if you work in sales and customer service settings, you can foster greater rapport with clientele by first repeating customers' verbalizations back to the customer, regardless of whether those verbalizations are in the form of questions, complaints, or even orders (e.g., "So, you're saying you'd *like to purchase ten units now with the possibility of increasing that to twenty units in May*").

The insight from this research was demonstrated in a less than desirable way when one of us was recently asked to review a series of recorded telephone conversations made to a customer service center. One rather angry customer called and demanded to speak to a manager because she was angry about a particular promise that this company had failed to act on.

"I'm sorry you're upset," came the reply from the customer service operator.

"I'm not upset, I'm angry," replied the customer in an increasingly loud voice.

"Yes, I can hear that you are disturbed."

"Disturbed? Disturbed? I am not disturbed, I am angry," shouted the customer.

The conversation quickly spiraled into a battle of wills with the customer becoming increasingly angry at the customer service agent's reluctance to acknowledge the fact that she was angry. The simple repetition of the customer's own words might have led to a different outcome.

"I'm sorry to hear that you are angry. What can we do together to resolve the situation?" would have been a more effective response and one that every one of us could apply to good effect when trying to build better rapport and stronger relationships.

32

What kind of smile can make the
world smile back?

D on't open a shop unless you like to smile," warns
a simple but instructive Chinese proverb. We've
all heard about the importance of service with a smile,
but is one smile the same as the next? And could the way
you smile have a positive effect on those who see it?

Social scientist Alicia Grandey and her colleagues
asked whether all types of smiles are equally effective
when it comes to customer satisfaction. Based on previous findings demonstrating that people can often distinguish between authentic and inauthentic smiles, the
research team thought that the authenticity of customer
service workers' smiles could have an influence on customer satisfaction, even though the difference between
the two types of smiles is very subtle.

In one study designed to test this possibility, the
researchers had participants watch one of several videos
of a customer service interaction between an employee
at the front desk of a hotel and a guest checking in at the
hotel; participants were also asked to indicate how satis-

fied they would feel with the interaction had they been the guest. Unbeknownst to the participants, the video was staged—the researchers hired actors to play the employee and the guest. Although the script between the actors remained the same, the researcher varied the instructions given to the actress playing the employee. In one case, she was asked to generate positive feelings toward the guest and to think about how she could make the guest feel good—the authentic condition. In the other case, she was told she was required to smile during the interaction—the inauthentic condition. The researchers also varied whether the hotel employee performed the tasks well or poorly. The first finding is an obvious one: The observers registered greater satisfaction when the hotel employee performed the tasks well versus poorly. A second finding was that when the tasks were performed poorly, authenticity of the smile didn't make much of a difference in reported satisfaction. However, when the tasks were performed well, those who viewed the "authentic smile" video said they would be more satisfied with the customer service than those who viewed the "inauthentic smile" video.

In a second study, one that took place in a more natural setting, the researchers surveyed random restaurant patrons about how satisfied they were with the customer service of the wait staff. In addition to asking about satisfaction, the patrons were asked about the perceived authenticity of the food servers' positive attitudes toward them. Consistent with the results of the other study, patrons who perceived their food servers to be authentic in their positive displays were more satisfied with their customer service.[59]

The results of this research suggest a revision of the old adage, "Smile and the world smiles with you." If you fake your smile, those you deal with may very well frown back. But how can we have, and encourage others to have, more authentically positive experiences?

One possibility for managers of service-oriented companies might be to provide emotional skills training to service workers to help them better regulate and elevate their moods. After all, unhappy employees, when forced to smile for their customers, may engage in lower-quality interactions, which will ultimately lead to reduced customer satisfaction. But that kind of emotional training often requires a great deal of time, effort, and cost.

A second, more general approach is to try to follow the wisdom of Benjamin Franklin: "Search others for their virtues." Many of us spend too much time finding faults in the people we deal with in our everyday lives. If, instead, we try to search their character for what we like about them, we'll like them more; and, as a result, they'll like us more. Everyone comes out ahead. This approach can also be fruitful in dealing with coworkers and superiors. One of us has a friend who had a very difficult relationship with her boss. They rarely saw eye to eye, but worse still, she truly disliked him as a person. One day, however, she decided to follow Franklin's advice. Even though her manager was not a kind person in the office, he was a very devoted family man, something she genuinely admired. After focusing on this quality, a little at a time, she started to like him more and more. One day, she told him that she admired how family-oriented he was, which she could say quite honestly. To her surprise, the next day, he was in her office, giving her a heads-up on some information that was very useful to her—an action she's certain he never would have taken before.

33

When is a loser a winner?

In the year 2003, there was clearly one car line that exceeded all U.S. sales projections to a far greater extent than any other. Ironically, this car line had previously proven itself to be a completely ineffective profit-maker for the manufacturer. Strange, then, that all of a sudden and without explanation, its sales skyrocketed. But why? It couldn't have been driven by advertising; in fact, because of disappointing sales, there was even less money available for marketing. Nor was there any engineering or price change to account for the unexpected popularity. Which car line was it, and why did it become so successful?

The car line was the Oldsmobile, and the reason for its success was paradoxical: General Motors, its manufacturer, had decided it was going to discontinue the line due to consistently poor sales. In response to the announcement that the Oldsmobile would soon no longer be available, sales jumped like never before. Why? The answer lies in the scarcity principle: People show a greater desire for an object or opportunity when they learn that it is unique, available in limited quantities, or obtainable for only a limited time.

Quite a bit of scientific research supports the power of scarcity to influence our decision-making. We can also see the scarcity principle operating in everyday life. In recent years, even the "holiday spirit" has become scarce, with parents practically fighting one another in stores for nearly-out-of-stock gaming consoles. In October 2003, the notion of losing something caused many thousands of people to stop their cars and block a major motorway just to see the final departure of the Concorde, a sight, it should be pointed out, that had been a familiar one every single day for the last thirty or so years. In fact, immediately after British Airways announced in February 2003 that it would be permanently grounding flights of the Concorde, the sale of seats on the plane did the opposite: They took off.

So what does this tell us about how to be more persuasive? If you run a business, you would be well advised to provide information to your customers about what is genuinely rare and unique about your products and services. Pointing out to them the features your product has that a competitor doesn't can be a powerful route to getting them to say yes to your offering and not your competition's. Similarly, colleagues at work might be persuaded to help you out on a project or initiative if they are told of its uniqueness: "It's not often we get the chance to be involved in an initiative such as this." Even family members are more likely to respond when told that your time and assistance are rare and dwindling. By simply and honestly pointing out that your products, services, time, and help are limited, you place a greater value on them, to the point that people appreciate them and you more. And, in general, we say yes more to those we appreciate.

We've all experienced the psychological effects of the scarcity principle in our daily lives. However, there is a less tangible domain in which the scarcity principle operates both subtly and powerfully: the domain of information. Studies have demonstrated that information that is exclusive is viewed as both more valuable and more persuasive. For example, in a study conducted by researcher Amram Knishinsky, wholesale beef buyers more than doubled their orders when they were informed that a shortage of Australian beef was likely due to weather conditions there—an understandable response in a competitive market. Yet, when those purchasers were told that the information came from an exclusive source and was not generally available to the rest of the public (both pieces of scarcity information were true), they increased their orders by a remarkable 600 percent![60]

These findings offer a clear insight and applications that will make your requests more persuasive. If you pass along information that is uniquely known by you, but fail to point out the exclusivity of the information, you could be losing an excellent opportunity to use an effective and ethical influence technique.

34

What can you gain from loss?

On April 23, 1985, the Coca-Cola Company made a decision that *Time* magazine later dubbed "the marketing fiasco of the decade." In response to data that more people preferred Pepsi's sweeter taste, they decided to pull their traditional formula for Coke off the market and replace it with a sweeter "New Coke." Many of us remember that day. In the words of one news report, "The Coca-Cola Company failed to foresee the sheer frustration and fury its action would create. From Bangor to Burbank, from Detroit to Dallas, tens of thousands of Coke lovers rose up as one to revile the taste of the new Coke and demand their old Coke back."[61]

Perhaps the most extreme example of this combined outrage and yearning comes from the story of a retired Seattle investor named Gay Mullins, who became something of a national celebrity by establishing a society called Old Cola Drinkers of America. This was a widespread group of people who worked tirelessly to get the traditional formula back on the market by using any civil, judicial, or legislative means available to them. For instance, he set up a hotline where angry consumers could vent their rage and register their feelings, which received over sixty thousand calls. He distributed anti-New Coke buttons and T-shirts by the thousands. And he even tried to bring a class-action lawsuit against the Coca-Cola Company, which was quickly dismissed by a federal judge. What's most astonishing about Mr. Mullins's behavior is that it didn't matter to him that in two separate blind taste tests, he either preferred New Coke over the original or couldn't tell the difference between them.

Note that the thing Mr. Mullins *liked more* was less valuable to him than the thing he felt he was *losing*. We'll come back to this idea in a moment. In the meantime, however, it's worth noting that even after giving in to customer demands and bringing the original Coke back to the shelves, company officials were stung and somewhat perplexed by what had hit them. As Donald Keough, then president of the Coca-Cola Company, said about consumers' diehard loyalty to the original Coke, "It's a wonderful American mystery, a lovely American enigma. And you can't measure it any more than you can measure love, pride, or patriotism."

We disagree. First off, it's no mystery, not if you understand the psychology of the scarcity principle, and particularly how it relates to people's sensitivity to losing something they already have. This is especially the case for a product that's as wrapped up in a person's history and traditions as Coca-Cola has always been throughout the world.

Second, this natural inclination on the part of Coca-Cola drinkers is not only something that *can* be measured, but something that we think the Coca-Cola Company *had* measured—in its own market research, no less. It was sitting right there in front of them before they made their infamous decision to change, but they hadn't combined their own data with an understanding of social influence factors.

The people of the Coca-Cola Company are no penny-pinchers when it comes to market research; they've been willing to spend hundreds of thousands of dollars—and more—to ensure that they've analyzed the market correctly for new products. In their decision to switch to the new Coke, they were no different. From 1981 to 1984, they very carefully tested the new and old formulas in taste tests involving nearly two hundred thousand people in twenty-five cities. What they found in their taste tests was a clear preference, 55 percent to 45 percent, for the *new* Coke over the old. Although most of these tests were blind, some of them were not conducted with unmarked samples. In those tests, the participants were told which was the old Coke and which was the new Coke beforehand. Under those conditions, the preference for the new Coke *increased* by an additional 6 percent.

How does that fit with the fact that people expressed a clear preference for the *old* Coke when the company finally introduced the new Coke? Consider the role scarcity played in each step of the timeline: During the taste tests, it was the new Coke that was unavailable to people for purchase, so, when they knew which sample was which, they showed an especially strong preference for what they couldn't otherwise have. The company must have looked at the 6 percent difference between blind and nonblind preferences and said to themselves, "Oh, good, this means that when people know *that they're getting something new,* their desire for it will shoot up." But, in fact, what that 6 percent increase really meant was that when people know *what it is they can't have,* their desire for it will shoot up. Later, when the company replaced the traditional recipe with the new one, now it was the old Coke that people couldn't have, and *it* became the favorite.

Even more powerfully than simply making a product unavailable, removing the original Coke from the shelves meant that, in the process, lifetime Coke drinkers were actually *losing* something they used to have regularly. The tendency to be more sensitive to possible losses than to possible gains is one of the best-supported findings in social science. Psychological researchers Daniel Kahneman and Amos Tversky were the first to test and document the notion of "loss aversion"—the idea that people are more motivated to avoid losses than they are to acquire gains. Loss aversion can explain quite a bit of human behavior, including behavior in areas such as finance, decision-making, negotiation, and persuasion.[62]

For example, one consequence of loss aversion is that it often motivates inexperienced investors to prematurely sell stocks that have gained in value because they simply don't want to lose what they've already gained. Similarly, the desire to avoid any potential for a loss also motivates these investors to hold on to stocks that have lost value since the date of purchase. Because selling the stock at that point would be to formally and irrevocably take a loss on the investment, many of these investors are reluctant to do so, a decision that often precedes further stock price decline.[63]

Loss aversion is also important from a marketing standpoint. Generally speaking, marketers and advertisers are often focused on getting the message out about the benefits of their product to potential customers. In attempting to do so, they often frame their message in terms of what the prospective clients have to gain from the product. In such cases, however, they may well be wasting an opportunity to present their message in an entirely more persuasive way by focusing on what the audience stands to lose in the situation. This suggests that rather than using language such as, "Take this opportunity to try our new product line at a 20 percent discount," one might be more successful using language such as, "Don't miss out on this opportunity to try our new product line at a 20 percent discount." In the latter example, you would be pointing out to the audience that because the deal is scarce in some way (e.g., limited time), they're in danger of genuinely losing the opportunity to purchase the products with the current discount.

Similarly, if you're hoping to persuade your colleagues to work with you on a particular project, it's important to point out not just what they stand to gain in terms of opportunities and experience but also that they stand to lose out on those very same factors. In fact, research has shown that potential losses figure far more heavily in managers' decision-making than the same things presented as gains. For example, let's say you have an idea that, if adopted, can potentially produce savings of up to one hundred thousand dollars a year for your department. Instead of presenting that idea as a saving, you're likely to be more persuasive if you frame the initiative in terms of losing the same amount if it fails to get adopted.[64]

It's also crucial to remember that you can be unduly influenced by this same strategy. For example, some devious negotiators—or even car salespeople—will wait until just before a final agreement appears to be within reach to throw in an unpalatable, take-it-or-leave-it demand, knowing full well that their counterparts are going to be disinclined to walk away; after all, walking away would mean a lot of lost time and effort and opportunity (also known as "sunk costs"). If you believe a salesperson with whom you're negotiating is manipulating your loss aversion in this way, you should walk away. It's the salesperson who should feel the loss.

35

Which single word will strengthen your persuasion attempts?

Based on L. Frank Baum's famous children's storybook, the 1939 film *The Wizard of Oz* remains today a traditional family favorite. Many of us are familiar with the plight of Dorothy and her friends the Scarecrow, the Tin Man, and the Lion as they make their perilous journey along the Yellow Brick Road. Clearly, the Wizard of Oz had succeeded in persuading them that he was both benevolent and powerful. After all, along the way, the four travelers say that they were off to see him "because because because because because of the wonderful things he does." What can their song tell us about how we can successfully persuade others to follow the paths we lay down for them?

Let's think about waiting in line. Whether you're at a bank, supermarket, or amusement park, waiting in line is probably not your idea of fun. Considering the almost universal motivation to get through the line as quickly as possible, under what circumstances would you be willing to let another person cut in front of you in the line? A central theme of this book is that small changes in the way that requests are made can often lead to some startlingly big results. But is it possible that just a single word from a requester could drastically increase the likelihood that you'd say, "Yes, go ahead"?

Yes—and the single word is *because*. Behavioral scientist Ellen Langer and her colleagues decided to put the persuasive power of this word to the test. In one study, Langer arranged for a stranger to approach someone waiting in line to use a photocopier and simply ask, "Excuse me, I have five pages. May I use the Xerox machine?" Faced with this direct request to cut ahead in the line, 60 percent of the people were willing to agree to allow the stranger to go ahead of them. However, when the stranger made the request with a *reason* ("May I use the Xerox machine, because I'm in a rush?"), almost everyone (94 percent) complied. This kind of boost may not seem very surprising. After all, providing a solid reason for the request justifies asking to jump ahead.

Here's where the study gets really interesting: Langer tested one more version of the request. This time, the stranger also used the word *because* but followed it with a completely meaningless reason. Specifically, the stranger said, "May I use the Xerox machine, because I have to make copies?" Because you have to *make copies*? Who doesn't? You're certainly not going to use it to sharpen your pencils, are you? Despite the hollowness of the "reason" the stranger provided, it generated nearly the same elevated levels of compliance as when the reason was wholly legitimate (93 percent).[65]

The Xerox study demonstrates the unique motivational influence of the word *because*. The word gets its persuasive power from the continually reinforced association over the course of our lives between *because* and the good rationales that typically follow it (e.g., " . . . because it would help me get that promotion," " . . . because I'm running out of time," " . . . because we have the best sports team money can buy").

Of course, like most things, the power of *because* has its limits. In the Xerox study, compliance was equally high no matter how poor the rationale was that followed *because*. But in those cases, the request was small—the requester only asked to make five copies. To see what would happen with a larger favor, Langer introduced another set of experimental conditions. The requester told a group of participants that she needed to make twenty copies. Besides the longer wait time, anyone who has ever used a copy machine knows the likelihood that the machine will jam seems to rise exponentially with each added page. In other words, participants' compliance with this larger request might have a substantially greater impact on them than compliance with a less involving request.

This time, when the stranger simply made her request without providing a reason or using the word *because,* only 24 percent complied. And for those who gave a bad reason (". . . because I need to make copies"), there was no increase in compliance at all. However, when the larger request was made with a good reason (" . . . because I'm in a hurry"), the response rate doubled. Taken together, the results of this study suggest that when the stakes are low, people are more likely to take mental shortcuts. On the other hand, when the stakes are high, people really do take the strength of the requester's reasoning into consideration when deciding how to respond to the request.

These findings serve as a reminder to always be sure to accompany your requests with a strong rationale, even when you think the reasons might be fairly clear. For example, when booking a meeting with a customer or when asking a coworker to cooperate on a new project, be sure to state the reasoning behind your request. That may sound obvious, but too often we mistakenly assume that other people understand the reasons behind our requests.

This strategy is also likely to pay dividends at home. Rather than demanding that your children "come to the table for dinner now," "do their homework," or "go to bed immediately," a more effective strategy would be to provide a reason why you are asking them to take that action—and not just "*because* I said so!"

It's important to note that the word *because* works both ways. You should not only say *because* to others, but also get others to say *because* to you. For instance, suppose that you work for an information technology services firm. Your long-term customers may have gotten used to working with your company over the years, and with each passing year, the actual reasons for sticking with your company may have become less salient, or even worse, may have been entirely forgotten. Consequently, your business can be left vulnerable to competitors. One effective way to strengthen your business ties and your clients' confidence in your company is to have the decision-makers at your client's firm generate a few reasons they use your business. This could be accomplished through formal or informal feedback surveys, in which the clients are asked to describe why they like doing business with your company. Research by Gregory Maio and colleagues suggests that this procedure will strengthen your clients' commitment to your firm by reminding the clients that the continued business relationship is rational rather than simply habitual. In other words, get people to say *because* to you, and like Dorothy and her travel companions, they'll end up singing your praises, too.[66]

36

When might asking for all the reasons be a mistake?

F irst, do no harm." Although the Hippocratic Oath applies first and foremost to medical practitioners' obligations to their patients, it surely holds for advertisers' obligations toward the products they are trying to sell. At the very least, they shouldn't *hurt* sales of the goods and services they're trying to sell. But how might a well-intentioned copywriter actually drive potential consumers of a given product away from that product and toward a competitor?

In the last chapter, we discussed how having people generate reasons that they're in favor of a certain position can be a highly effective strategy for strengthening their beliefs in that position. If we apply this thinking to advertisements, it seems wise to encourage consumers to think of as many reasons as possible to choose our goods and services. However, recent research suggests that under certain circumstances, this strategy can actually backfire.

Imagine you're in the market for a new premium automobile, and you've narrowed your choices down to either a BMW or a Mercedes. You open a magazine and see an ad for BMW that says the following:

> BMW or Mercedes? There are many reasons to choose a BMW. Can you name 10?

In one study conducted by Michaela Wänke and her colleagues, a group of business students saw an ad just like this among several other advertisements. A different group of business students at the same university saw a slightly different ad—one that stated, "BMW or Mercedes? There are many reasons to choose a BMW. Can you name *one*?" (emphasis added).

Afterward, the participants were asked for their opinions about BMW and Mercedes, including their interest in one day purchasing a vehicle from either of those brands. The results were clear: The advertising copy that asked readers to name ten reasons to choose a BMW led to *lower* evaluations of the BMW and higher evaluations of the Mercedes than the copy that asked the readers to name just one reason to choose a BMW.

What's responsible for this backfire effect? The researchers explain that participants in this study based their judgments of BMW on how easy they found it to come up with reasons in support of BMW. When they were asked to name only one reason, participants had a relatively easy time coming up with a single advantage. However, when they were asked to name ten, the task was hard. They might have identified a few such reasons rather easily, but they found the process of coming up with so many reasons to be difficult. So, rather than using the *number* of reasons they generated as the best indicator for their evaluations of the brands, the participants instead based their judgments on the *ease or difficulty* of the process of generating reasons. More generally, psychologists refer to the ease or difficulty of experiencing something as the "fluency" of that experience, a concept we'll be coming back to.[67]

The data from this research indicate that before asking your audience to generate many reasons in support of your position, it's important to consider just how easily they'll be able to do so. If the task seems like a relatively difficult one, ask them instead to generate only a small number of reasons. The findings also suggest a rather ironic strategy: You can potentially give yourself a competitive edge by asking your audience to generate many reasons *in favor of your rival's offerings*. The more difficult it is for the audience to come up with a large number of rationales, the better your goods, services, or initiatives will look in comparison.

Other research has shown that the ease or difficulty of merely *imagining* using a product will also affect consumers' decisions. With lead researcher Petia Petrova, one of us conducted a series of studies showing that encouraging customers to imagine themselves experiencing the delights of a restaurant or holiday destination only increases the desire to visit *if it's easy to imagine doing so*.[68]

Along these lines, one aspect you might want to consider is the extent to which your product, or more generally, your request for the behavior you'd like your audience to undertake, involves actions that are novel or foreign to them. For instance, you may want to persuade a consumer group to purchase a brand-new product marketed by your company. If this product has complicated technical features with which the group has little to no experience and that have not yet been fully explained, it may be difficult for your prospects to imagine themselves actually using the product, which will make them less likely to select it.

Another arena where these findings are clearly important is in advertising production. Art directors are often given free rein to generate images that are eye-catching or memorable, but in the process, they may create pictures that are abstract, giving little consideration to how their images affect the target audience's ability to visualize themselves using the featured product. This research shows that concrete images are likely to be more effective than abstract ones. In addition, the decision-making process in these types of cases can be facilitated through greater collaboration with the copywriters, prior testing of the ads, and focus groups that are specifically geared toward understanding how easy or difficult it is for a relevant audience to imagine themselves in the requested situations.

37

How can the simplicity of a name make it appear more valuable?

When he was once asked the complex question of what the stock market would do next, J. P. Morgan reportedly gave a simple response: "It will fluctuate." But how can the power of simplicity–particularly in the naming of your product, your project, or even your company–help you boost your influence and exceed your own earnings expectations?

According to social scientists Adam Alter and Daniel Oppenheimer, people tend to have a greater affection for words and names that are easy to pronounce (that is, those that have a high degree of fluency) than those that are hard to pronounce. They argued that people would feel more positively toward company names and stock symbols that are relatively easy to read and to pronounce, leading to higher stock prices.

To first test this hypothesis in a controlled study, they generated names of fictitious stocks that were either very easy to pronounce or very difficult to pronounce. They told study participants that these were real companies and asked them to estimate the future performance of each of the stocks. The results were clear: Not only did participants predict that the easily pronounceable stocks (e.g., Slingerman, Vander, Tanley) would outperform the others (e.g., Sagxter, Frurio, Xagibdan), they also predicted the latter would go down, while the former would rise.

To find out if this effect happened in the real world, Alter and Oppenheimer randomly picked eighty-nine companies whose shares were traded on the New York Stock Exchange and had their initial public offering between 1990 and 2004. They then looked at the relationship between the fluency of a stock name and its performance one day, one week, six months, and one year after the initial public offering for that stock. The researchers found that if a person invested a thousand dollars in the ten most fluently named companies on the list versus the ten least fluently named companies on the list, the investment in the first group would have outperformed its counterpart for each of the designated time periods, including a $333 difference just one year after the initial public offering. What's more, in a separate study, the authors separated over 750 companies listed on the New York Stock Exchange or the American Stock Exchange by whether their stock ticker symbol was pronounceable (e.g., KAR) or unpronounceable (e.g., RDO). They found similar results.[69]

So, are we recommending that you go right out and trade in your shares of Mxyzptlk Holding Corp. for Yahoo! stock, fire your financial advisor, or have a garage sale to rid yourself of your stock-picking monkeys and dartboards? Not quite. However, we are advising you not to underestimate the power of simplicity, even in the name you give your company, product, or initiative. Often, people are so focused on seemingly more influential aspects of their projects that they overlook the first piece of information that will be communicated to its audience—its name. All else being equal, the easier it is to read and pronounce, the more likely consumers, potential stockholders, and other decision-makers will be to view it positively.

In a similar vein, researchers have found that the persuasiveness of a handwritten message is influenced by the quality of the handwriting: The worse the handwriting, the less persuasive the message will be. Readers mistakenly interpret the sense of difficulty they feel when they read a message with bad handwriting as a sense of difficulty believing the content of the message. At least on the surface of things, there appears to be an easy and accessible solution for those of us who are calligraphically challenged: Can't we just type out our persuasive messages? Yes, but even that advice comes with a caveat: Research has demonstrated that your arguments are likely to be deemed far more persuasive if they are in an easy-to-read font.

The findings of all this research also have more general implications for how people choose to communicate with one another. Take, for example, the fact that communicators frequently try to convey their erudition via their grandiloquent, magniloquent, sesquipedalian verbosity; in other words, they try to look smart by using unnecessarily long words or overly technical jargon.* Consider, for instance, the following communication sent out by a manager to his team as reported in the *New York Post* in October 2006:

> We're leveraging our assets and establishing strategic alliances to create a robust knowledge center— one with a customer-ruled business structure using market-leading technologies to maximize our human systems.[70]

Huh? This apparently means, "We're consultants." Additional research by Oppenheimer has shown that using overly complex language like this can produce the exact opposite of the intended effect: Because the audience has difficulty interpreting the language, the message is deemed less convincing and the author is perceived to be less intelligent. [71]

Regrettably, these kinds of messages are all too frequent in everyday life, ranging from business communications to health care advice to the language used in students' papers. For example, a poll taken at Stanford University found that 86.4 percent of the students surveyed admitted they had used complicated language in their academic essays to try to make themselves sound smarter. More disturbing, however, is the finding from a U.K.-based consulting services firm that 56 percent of employees thought that their managers and supervisors didn't communicate clearly with them and often used

---

*Something we would never do, of course.

incomprehensible language that confused the messages, making them generally less persuasive. If you make sure your message is clear and simple, the people who receive it might not throw a ticker tape parade in your honor, but at the very least, they won't sell your information short.

38

How can rhyme make your influence climb?

I s Gillette really the best a man can get? Are loose lips responsible for sinking ships? Is it true that the best part of waking up is Folgers in your cup? When it comes to seat belts, will I really get a ticket if I don't click it? And finally, compared to its competitors, is Bounty truly the quilted, thicker, quicker, picker-upper?

From advertising to public service announcements, rhyming slogans are everywhere. Out of all the potential marketing strategies to choose from, why do so many organizations convey their message with rhymes? Part of it is that rhyming messages are more memorable and easily repeated to others, which should come as no surprise. But could it also be that rhyming statements are actually seen as more accurate and truthful?

Noting the pervasiveness of rhyming proverbs such as "Birds of a feather flock together," social scientists Matthew McGlone and Jessica Tofighbakhsh set out to investigate whether statements that rhyme are thought to be more accurate than those that don't. As part of their study, they took a number of rhyming sayings previously unknown to the study participants and created parallel but nonrhyming versions of them. For example, they took the relatively obscure saying, "Caution and measure will win you treasure," and modified it to say, "Caution and measure will win you riches." As another example, they took the saying, "What sobriety conceals, alcohol reveals," and changed it to, "What sobriety conceals, alcohol unmasks."

Participants then read some of these sayings and rated each one for the extent to which it accurately reflects the way the world really works. The researchers found that even though all the participants in the study strongly held the belief that rhyming was in no way an indicator of accuracy, they nonetheless perceived the statements that rhymed as more accurate than those that didn't.

The researchers explained that rhyming phrases are characterized by greater processing fluency: They're mentally processed more easily than nonrhyming phrases. Because people tend to base accuracy evaluations, at least partly, on the perceived fluency of the incoming information, the rhyming statements are actually judged as more accurate.[72]

These findings have many applications in everyday life. For one, the results of this research suggest that when marketers and business operators think about what slogans, mottos, trademarks, and jingles to employ, they should consider that using rhymes may increase not only the likability of the message, but also its perceived truthfulness. Perhaps this is why, when asked what a company could say about its product when there was nothing new to say about it, a seasoned advertising executive replied,

"Well, if you have nothing to say about your product, then I suppose you can always sing about it."

Second, parents can use rhyme to their advantage when faced with a common and frustrating influence challenge—getting their kids to go to bed. After quality time reading nursery rhymes with them, perhaps having them join in a few verses of "It's off to bed for sleepyhead" will prove persuasive.

Finally, the power of rhyme can even be applied in a legal setting. In fact, the authors of this research point out one infamous rhyme that seems so weighty that it just may have tipped the scales of justice. During O. J. Simpson's murder trial, Johnnie Cochran, Simpson's defense attorney, told the jury, "If the gloves don't fit, you must acquit!" Considering the subtle influence of rhyme, the study's authors may be right to question how the verdict might have been affected if Cochran had instead implored, "If the gloves don't fit, you must find him not guilty!"

39

What can batting practice tell us about persuasion?

The world of sports can be a useful training ground for those of us who wish to become more persuasive. At a baseball game it's relatively common to see players place a weighted ring around their bat before they take their warm-up swings. According to the ballplayers, repeatedly swinging a heavier bat makes the unweighted bat feel lighter in comparison.

The primary principle underlying this effect is known as perceptual contrast. Simply put, the characteristics of objects are not perceived in a vacuum, but rather in comparison to others. If you are asked to pick up a ten-pound weight in a gymnasium, it will appear lighter if you had first picked up a twenty-pound weight and heavier if you had first picked up a five-pound weight. Nothing has actually changed about the ten-pound weight—except your perception of it. This psychological process is not limited to weight; it holds for almost any type of judgment you could make. In every case the perceptual process is the same: Prior experience colors perception.

Social psychologists Zakary Tormala and Richard

Petty recently applied these principles to show how contrast effects can influence the persuasion process. Specifically, they looked at how the *amount of information* people think they have about something can be influenced by the amount of information they learn about something else. These researchers asked people to read a persuasive message for a fictitious department store (the "target message") called Brown's, but only after reading a persuasive message for a different fictitious department store ("the prior message") called Smith's. The target message was the same for all participants of the experiment—it described three departments of Brown's. The prior message varied, with less (one department) or greater (six departments) information about Smith's. When the prior message contained a great deal of information, the target message was seen as less persuasive and produced less favorable attitudes toward the department store, whereas the opposite occurred when the prior message contained very little information. It seems that the participants felt more knowledgeable about Brown's after learning relatively little about Smith's, and vice versa. This is the perceptual contrast effect in action.

To extend their findings, the researchers conducted another study that was similar in most respects to the first one. However, before receiving persuasive information about another department store, they received a little or a lot of persuasive information about a car (the Mini Cooper). The results were consistent with the earlier study, suggesting that the prior information doesn't even need to be all that relevant to affect the persuasive impact of a subsequent message.[73]

This idea can be applied to sales. Imagine that you work for a company selling a line of products, and you're confident that one particular product would provide the best fit for your prospective client. You should be sure to discuss the merits of that better-fitting product at length after you've spent a much shorter period of time discussing another product.

What's interesting to note is that perceptual contrast offers us a very efficient means of persuasion. Often we don't have the luxury of changing our products, services, or offerings—it would be far too costly and time-consuming. But using perceptual contrast, we can change how others think about our initiatives, goods, services, and requests. To give just one real-world example, a home improvement company was able to increase the sales of one of its top-of-the-range backyard hot tubs by over 500 percent simply by (a) telling prospective customers, honestly, that many buyers of the top-of-the-range model reported that having it was like adding an extra room to the house and then (b) asking them to consider how much it would cost to build another room onto the side of their house. After all, a fifteen-thousand-dollar spa seems much less expensive when compared with construction that would cost at least twice as much.

40

How can you get a head start in the quest for loyalty?

Whether it's free cups of coffee, money-off vouchers, discounted flights, or coupons toward your next hotel stay, many companies look to increase customer loyalty by offering incentive programs such as frequent flyer plans and clubcard point programs. The results of some recent research offer insights into how you can increase interest in what you have to offer and strengthen the loyalty of your customers.

Consumer researchers Joseph Nunes and Xavier Dreze thought that customers involved in an incentive program would show more loyalty to the company by reaching payoff milestones more quickly if given a head start by the company—even without decreasing the amount of purchases needed to reach the reward.

In one study, loyalty cards were handed out to three hundred customers of a local car wash. The customers were told that every time they had their car washed, their loyalty card would be stamped. However, there were two types of cards. One type of card required eight stamps to receive a free car wash, with no stamps attached to the card. The other stated that ten stamps were needed to receive the free wash, but two stamps were already affixed to the card. This meant that both cards required eight washes to receive the reward, but the second group seemed well on its way to completing the card with 20 percent of the stamps needed for the free wash.

Afterward, every time a customer came back for another wash, an employee affixed a stamp to the card and recorded the date. After several months, when the researchers ended the program and looked at the data, their hypotheses had been confirmed: Whereas only 19 percent of customers in the eight-stamp group made enough visits to claim their free car wash, 34 percent of the ten-stamp, head-start group did. What's more, the head-start group took less time to complete their eighth purchase, taking an average of 2.9 fewer days between visits to the car wash.

According to Nunes and Dreze, reframing the program as one that's been started but not completed rather than as one that has not yet begun meant that people felt more motivated to complete it. They also pointed to research showing that the closer people get to completing a goal, the more effort they exert to achieve that goal. The data revealed that the amount of time between visits decreased by about half a day on average with every additional car wash that was purchased.[74]

Besides the application of these findings to loyalty programs of all sorts, the results of this study indicate that when soliciting another person for help on anything, you should try to point out how that person has already taken steps toward the completion of that task. For example, if you need help on a project that's similar to one that a colleague has worked on in the past, you can emphasize that, in essence, she is well on her way to finishing the assignment. And if you've already done a fair amount of work on the project, you can underscore that the task is already almost 30 percent completed. In this way, your colleague is more likely to view the project as one that's already underway but incomplete rather than as one that she has to start from scratch.

For another example, suppose you are a sales manager. Your sales team has a target of a certain number of sales, but the team isn't doing too well in the early stages. You learn that a large sale to be processed centrally is already in the offing. Rather than keeping the information about this sale to yourself, thinking that you might use it to fall back on if your team doesn't hit the target, you should consider publicizing this sale. In this way, you'd present a progressive effect toward the goal, promoting even more sales.

Educators and parents can also benefit from such a strategy. Imagine that your child is being particularly stubborn about doing his homework and you feel compelled to try incentives. If you decide to give him one full Saturday at the zoo for every six weekends in which he does his homework, you might find that he would be especially motivated to comply if you started him off with "credit" for one weekend before your little program officially begins.

The message is clear: People will be more likely to stick with programs and tasks if you can first offer them some evidence of how they've already made progress toward completing them. If you use this strategy, like cars at a car wash, your influence will sparkle.

41

What can a box of crayons teach us about persuasion?

Gone are the days when the names of colors were simple. Anyone who opens a new box of crayons will quickly notice that the old common names (e.g., green, yellow, brown) have been replaced by names such as Tropical Rain Forest, Laser Lemon, and Fuzzy Wuzzy Brown. How can a color name like Cornflower or Razzmatazz help you keep your company's chips blue and your business out of the red?

Researchers Elizabeth Miller and Barbara Kahn noticed this aspect of crayons and countless other products, and sought to better understand how these kinds of differences in product names influence consumer preferences. As part of their research they distinguished between four categories of color and flavor names:

1. Common, which are typical and unspecific (e.g., blue);

2. Common descriptive, which are typical and specific (e.g., sky blue);

3. Unexpected descriptive, which are atypical and specific (e.g., Kermit green); and

4. Ambiguous, which are atypical and unspecific (e.g., millennium orange).

The researchers thought that unexpected descriptive (3) and ambiguous (4) color and flavor names should elicit more positive feelings toward a given product than the other two types (1 and 2) of color and flavor names. However, they believed that these two types of names are effective for different reasons. Unexpected descriptive names, such as Kermit green, are effective because they act as a sort of puzzle to be solved, which typically leads people to consider more aspects of the products–particularly the positive ones. Although solving this little puzzle may not qualify consumers to join Mensa, it may create an "aha!" moment that could lead them to associate positive emotions with the product. Ambiguous names, such as millennium orange, prompt consumers to try to discover, in the absence of any meaningful information, what the makers of the product were trying to convey with that name. This also leads consumers to think about the positive aspects the company is trying to highlight with the name. Using a variety of names for jelly bean flavors and for sweater colors, Miller and Kahn confirmed that products with unexpected descriptive and ambiguous names were in fact regarded as more desirable than were those of the other two category types.[75]

What are the implications for a business looking to develop names or descriptions of its products and services? One answer would be that businesses should not shy away from using less-than-straightforward names for certain aspects of its products.* Names that fall into the unexpected descriptive category or the ambiguous category create a sense of mystery and intrigue that leads potential customers to consider the positive aspects of your goods and services. In fact, this approach doesn't just have to work for products and services. Let's say, for example, that you're looking to gain resources from colleagues at work to support a new project or training initiative. By using what might be considered an unexpected title or name for the project, or even adopting an ambiguous one, you might well foster a sense of fascination with and attraction to it.

We can also put the lessons of this research into practice at home. For instance, when our kids are considering whether to go out for dinner with their friends or eat at home, jazzing up the label we give tonight's supper (e.g., "chicken surprise" instead of plain old "chicken") may very well convince them to stay at home with us for the night. Of course, when we'd rather have a quiet night at home, responding with "broccoli and cod liver oil stew" instead is always an option . . .

---

*Note that these less-than-straightforward names should still be easily readable and pronounceable, as we discussed in a previous chapter.

42

How can you package your message to ensure it keeps going, and going, and going?

Who am I? I'm pink. I'm a toy rabbit. I have a drum. And I'm powered by a brand-name battery that outlasts the competition. Who am I?

Depending on where you live, I'm either the Energizer Bunny or the Duracell Bunny. Confused yet? You're not alone.

The very first pink, battery-powered bunny with a penchant for persistent percussion on television was actually the Duracell Bunny. To be more accurate, it wasn't a single bunny, but rather a whole species of toy rabbits—the Duracell Bunnies—whose power was said to be longer-lasting than that of any other brand of battery. In one commercial, for instance, a number of drum-beating toy rabbits, each powered by a different brand of battery, slowly come to a standstill, leaving only one—the one powered by Duracell—still literally full of energy.

Over fifteen years ago, however, Duracell failed to renew its trademark in the United States, which allowed its competitor, Energizer, to swoop in and trademark its own pink, alkaline-powered drumming bunny in an effort to mock the Duracell campaign and claim its products' superiority. This is why, these days, North American television viewers are accustomed to seeing their bunnies running on Energizer, whereas it's Duracell for those in the rest of the world.

In the Energizer television commercials, viewers think they are watching an advertisement for another product (Sitagain Hemorrhoid Ointment, for example), which is interrupted by the Energizer Bunny walking through the frame to the narration of, " . . . still going, and going, and going, and going . . . nothing outlasts the Energizer." Despite the early public and critical acclaim that these commercials received for the Energizer Bunny's off-the-wall and into-other-commercial antics, there was just one problem: Many people, even those who loved the commercials, couldn't remember which company's batteries were being advertised. In fact, one survey showed that, even out of viewers who chose the bunny ads as their favorite commercials of the year, an astonishing 40 percent were certain that the ads were for Duracell. This was the case even though there are plenty of features that distinguished the Energizer Bunny from its coppertop counterpart, including bigger ears, sunglasses, a larger drum, fur that's a brighter shade of pink, and flip-flops.

Confusion between the two companies' bunnies certainly played a role in this problem. But, as it turns out, even many people who'd never seen the Duracell commercials misremembered which brand sponsored these newer commercials, thinking it was Duracell. In fact, shortly after the ads became popular, it was *Duracell's* market share that grew, while Energizer's shrunk a bit.[76]

What action should Energizer have taken to prevent such a problem from occurring in the first place, and what lessons can we learn from it? The psychological research is clear: Placing a memory aid on store displays and the actual packaging of their product—for example, an image of the Energizer Bunny with the text "Keeps going and going and going . . ."—would do much to correct consumers' faulty memories as well as product choices that they made based on those incorrect memories. And that's exactly what the company eventually did, with great success.

What's the implication for marketing in general? Increasingly, companies try to brand themselves via extensive media campaigns that emphasize the key element of their brand (e.g., durability or quality or economy) through a story character that epitomizes that element. They assume that viewers will connect their products with the branded element while exposed to the ads, which is a reasonable assumption provided that the ads are properly constructed. They also assume that viewers will recall the connection when ready to buy—and that's a naïve assumption. Consumers' memories, subjected to hundreds of thousands of these associations in the course of modern life, aren't up to the task—at least not without the assistance of point-of-purchase cues that revive the desired connection. It's for this reason that any major advertising campaign needs to integrate the essential images, characters, or slogans of the ads into the in-store product displays and product packaging the consumer sees when making a purchase choice. Although changing the display and packaging to match the central features of the media campaign may be more expensive in the short term, it's essential.[77]

This strategy isn't limited to marketing products; it can also be used to market information and ideas. Consider, for example, the massive challenge you'd face if you were part of a health organization devoted to reducing alcohol abuse on university campuses. Even if you were capable of creating an advertising campaign that motivates students to drink less, how would you ensure that the message stays on their minds when it's most necessary?

To take an example, one type of persuasion campaign that's become increasingly popular with university health administrators who are trying to battle student alcohol abuse has been dubbed "social norms marketing." Researchers have found that students typically overestimate the number of drinks that their peers consume, and as we know from our discussions of social proof, people are motivated to behave in line with perceived social norms. The goal of social norms marketing campaigns is to reduce the frequency of college student alcohol abuse by correcting students' misperceptions. For example, a social norms marketing poster might indicate that a survey found that "65 percent of students at our university have three or fewer drinks when they party." The thinking is that providing the poster's readers with more accurate figures for the amount that their peers drink will reduce the amount that they'll want to drink when they party.

Although these programs certainly show signs of promise, the current evidence for their success is mixed. Even though such posters may be somewhat persuasive when students actually read them, perhaps one of the reasons that these campaigns are not more effective is that by the time the students get to situations in which drinking occurs, they either forget about or aren't focused on that information. For instance, posters, signs, and other forms of media conveying anti-alcohol messages in normative campaigns are commonly (and understandably, from a practical point of view) placed in libraries, classrooms, student unions, health centers, and common areas of residence halls rather than the settings in which drinking is most likely to occur. Unfortunately, the disconnect between where students see the information and where they are when they drink means that the distant voice of the message is likely to be drowned out by the here-and-now sounds of clanking bottles and drunken laughter prevalent in bars, clubs, parties, and residence halls.[78]

The memory aid research indicates that students' likelihood of focusing on the social norms information in the appropriate settings could be strengthened by placing the campaign's logo on objects native to those settings (e.g., coasters, entrance bracelets, hand stamps). Alternatively, the campus could give away items that have the campaign's logo imprinted on it, such as Frisbees. Students in that case would be likely to take them back to their dorm rooms or fraternity houses where they would be more likely to see the memory aid. Ironically, this strategy might even be more effective once the students get some alcohol in them, as some research shows that simple persuasive messages tend to be more successful when people are drinking.[79] In a similar approach, some communities have tried to fight drunk driving by getting participating bar owners to put into patrons' drinks something called "light cubes," which are LED lights enclosed in plastic in the shape of ice cubes. Emitting flashes of red and blue light, these memory aids typically have the effect of making the drink look like flashing blue and red police car lights, serving as a persuasive extension of the long arm of the law.

All in all, using memory aids will assure that your message doesn't fade at the finish, but keeps going and going and going . . .

43

What object can persuade people to reflect on their values?

M irror, mirror, on the wall, what's one of the most persuasive objects of them all? Actually, mirror, you are.

No one doubts that the primary purpose of a mirror is to allow us to see what we look like on the outside, but mirrors also act as windows into what we look like—and perhaps more important, what we *want* to look like—on the inside. As a result, looking at ourselves in a mirror causes us to reflect on our behavior and act in more socially desirable ways.

Take, for example, a study conducted on Halloween by social scientist Arthur Beaman and his colleagues. Rather than conducting their study in a university laboratory or on the street, Beaman temporarily converted eighteen local houses into makeshift research facilities. When trick-or-treaters rang the doorbell of one of the houses involved in the study, a research assistant greeted them, asked them their names, and then pointed to a large bowl of candy sitting on a nearby table. After telling the children that they could each take *one* of the candies, she mentioned that she had some work to do and quickly exited the room. That part of the experiment was the treat. And here's the trick: What the children didn't know, besides the fact that they were in a cleverly devised experiment, was that someone was secretly watching them through a hidden peephole. That person was another research assistant who had the job of recording whether each child behaved honestly by taking only one piece of candy.

When the results were in, the data revealed that over a third of the kids took more candy than they should have—33.7 percent, to be exact. But, as we've already hinted, the researchers wanted to see if they could use a mirror to reduce the rate of candy theft. In these cases, the research assistant angled a large mirror by the candy bowl in such a way that the trick-or-treaters had to look at themselves in the mirror when they took the candy. The theft rate when the mirror was present? Only 8.9 percent.[80]

In a similar vein, one of us conducted a study examining how focusing people on themselves and their own image makes them act more consistently with their values. Led by behavioral scientist Carl Kallgren, we first assessed participants' feelings about littering at the beginning of an academic semester. Later in the semester, when participants arrived at the laboratory, half were exposed to a closed-circuit television featuring their own image (so that it was almost like seeing themselves in a mirror), while the other half watched a closed-circuit television featuring geometric shapes. They were told that they would be completing a task that required their heart rate to be monitored, which involved placing some gel on their hand. Once the subjects believed they were done with the study, a research assistant handed them a paper towel to wipe off the gel and asked them to exit through the stairwell located on that floor. We were looking to see whether each participant dropped the paper towel in the stairwell on his or her way toward the exit.

What we found is that when they hadn't viewed an image of themselves before they had the opportunity to litter, about 46 percent of the participants littered. But when they had, only about 24 percent littered. If there's one thing this study does, it helps answer the question, "How can people who litter look at themselves in the mirror every day?" The answer appears to be that they don't.[81]

In everyday life, we can use mirrors to persuade others in the most subtle manner to behave in more socially desirable ways. Besides telling us how to arrange our Halloween treats, this research indicates that carefully placed mirrors can encourage kids to act more kindly toward one another. Also, a manager who has experienced employee theft—in the organization's stockroom, for example—might find that mirrors do wonders to reduce stealing. In this case, mirrors act as a good alternative to video surveillance, which is not only costly, but sends a signal to the employees that they're not trusted—a prospect that can actually lead to greater employee theft down the line, not less.[82]

If adding mirrors to a specific location isn't practical, there are two other possibilities that produce mirror-like effects. First, social psychologist Ed Diener and his colleagues have found that asking people their names can have a similar effect. This means that asking kids and employees alike to wear name tags should lay the groundwork for more desirable behavior.[83] Second, recent research by scientist Melissa Bateson and colleagues suggests that placing a simple picture of eyes on the wall also has the effect of getting others to act in more socially conscious ways. For instance, in one study, the researchers added a picture to a communal area where various staff members are supposed to pay for their coffee or tea consumption. In other words, if they drink coffee or tea, they're supposed to drop a certain amount of money into a jar to pay for it. But the pictures changed each week: One week, the picture was flowers, the next week it was eyes, then a different set of flowers, then a new set of eyes, and so forth. The results showed that coffee and tea drinkers paid over 2.5 times more for their drink when the sign was accompanied by a picture of a pair of eyes than when it was accompanied by a picture of flowers.[84]

As these findings demonstrate, it can't hurt to have another pair of eyes looking over the situation, regardless of whether they're yours or someone else's.

44

Does being sad make your negotiations bad?

I n one episode of the hugely successful television series *Sex and the City*, the main character, Carrie Bradshaw, is walking down a New York City street with close friend Samantha Jones, who is telling Carrie why she's felt so sad recently. Samantha is walking with a noticeable limp. At one point in the conversation, Samantha exclaims, "Ow!" In response, Carrie enquires, "Honey, if it hurts so much, why are we going shopping?" Samantha retorts, "I have a broken toe, not a broken spirit."[85]

Each year, millions of us who feel down try to alleviate our sorrow through shopping. A recent study conducted by social psychologist Jennifer Lerner and her colleagues investigated how emotions such as sadness can deeply affect people's buying—and selling—behavior, providing us with some interesting insights about the prevalence of this phenomenon.

The researchers hypothesized that the experience of sadness activates the motivation in people to alter their circumstances, which might help them change their mood and get them out of their funk. They also thought that this motivation would affect buyers and sellers in different ways: Sad buyers would be willing to pay a higher price for a given item than neutral buyers, whereas sad sellers would part with the same item for a lower price than neutral sellers.

In an experiment designed to test these ideas, the researchers induced either sadness or no emotion in their participants by having them view one of two different film clips. Those assigned to the sadness-inducing condition watched a movie clip from the film *The Champ,* which featured the death of a boy's mentor; following that, they were asked to write a brief paragraph about how they'd feel if they'd been in the situation portrayed in the clip. Those assigned to the no-emotion condition watched an emotionally neutral film clip featuring fish and then wrote about their day-to-day activities. Afterward, all participants were told that they were about to take part in a second, unrelated study. Some of the participants were given a set of highlighters and asked to set a price at which to sell them, whereas the other half were asked to set a price at which they would buy the very same item.

The results supported Lerner's assertions. Sad buyers were willing to purchase the item for around 30 percent *more* than were emotionally neutral buyers. And sad sellers were willing to part with the item for around 33 percent *less* than were their emotionally neutral counterparts. What's more, the researchers found that the carryover of the emotion from the movie into their economic decisions occurred completely outside of the subjects' awareness—they had no idea they had been so deeply affected by these residual feelings of sadness.[86]

It's not just the negative emotions that can affect our decision-making tendencies. Behavioral scientists Christopher Hsee and Yuval Rottenstreich have asserted that people's judgment and decision-making abilities can be impaired by any emotionally charged issue, regardless of the positivity or negativity of the feelings it produces. They argue that emotions lead people to become less sensitive to differences in the *magnitude of numbers*; in other words, people are more likely to pay attention to the simple *presence or absence* of an event as opposed to the specific numbers that characterize the event. What this means is that people are more likely to pay attention to the simple presence or absence of an emotion-laden offer as opposed to the specific numbers that characterize the offer.

To test this idea, the researchers asked participants to spend a brief period of time thinking about some issues either emotionally or nonemotionally. Shortly afterward, these research subjects were told to imagine that someone they knew was selling a set of Madonna CDs. Half of them were told that there were a total of five CDs in the bundle, whereas the other half of the participants were told that there were a total of ten CDs in the bundle. Participants were then asked to report the maximum amount they'd be willing to pay for the bundle of CDs.

The researchers found that those who had earlier spent time thinking in an unemotional manner were willing to pay more for the set of ten CDs than for the set of five CDs, a decision-making outcome that's quite rational. More interestingly, however, those who had earlier practiced thinking in an emotional manner were insensitive to the magnitude difference in number of CDs, reporting that they would pay roughly the same amounts for the set of ten CDs as they would for the set of five CDs.[87]

The results of this study suggest that emotional experiences can have a detrimental impact on decision-making, perhaps allowing you to be persuaded by an offer when you shouldn't be. Suppose that you are negotiating with a supplier for raw materials, and there is a ten-thousand-dollar gap between the amount of money you are offering and the quantity of the raw materials the supplier is willing to provide to you for that amount. Recognizing this disparity, but not willing to provide any more of those raw materials for the amount of money you're offering, the supplier might offer to throw in fifty units of a brand-new product that you might be excited about due to its novelty. Whereas it may be the case that a hundred units, not fifty, are roughly valued at ten thousand dollars, this research teaches us that offers laden with emotion such as this one could potentially lead the buyer to overestimate the value of the fifty units, and thus make a poor and unprofitable decision.

The same is true when buying a car, a process that's invariably a roller coaster of emotions. After you've picked out your new beauty, it may be the case that what you're willing to buy it for and what the salesperson is willing to sell it for is off by five hundred dollars. Knowing full well how much you want the car and how emotional you are in the moment, salespeople will try to throw in an additional item, such as a set of mud flaps, whose value is realistically nowhere near five hundred dollars.

How can we prevent these factors from influencing us? The findings from this study indicate that doing something as simple as focusing on numbers and calculations before the negotiation should help restore your ability to differentiate between the magnitudes of numbers. It might even behoove you to come prepared with a pricing sheet and a calculator in hand, and always keep them in front of you on the table.

More generally, though, it's extremely important to recognize what emotional state or mood you are in before you make an important decision, begin a crucial negotiation, or even respond to an unfriendly or aggressive email. For example, suppose you have the task of negotiating the financial terms of your contract with a vendor. If you've just gone through an emotional experience, even though you might think your decision-making ability would be unaffected, you should consider holding off on the negotiation process. This short delay will allow time for those emotions to subside, allowing you to make more rational choices.

Even if you're not experiencing a particularly acute emotional feeling, it would generally be good practice in any high-value decision-making situation to allow a period of time to pass, to compose yourself. Often, people schedule meetings back to back as a matter of convenience. However, by giving yourself a short break between meetings, you'll reduce the likelihood that the feelings generated by an emotionally charged meeting don't spill over into the next—especially if the second meeting is one in which you'll need to make budget or purchasing decisions.

The same is true with decisions that you might make at home. You might be considering the purchase of some new furniture, a new appliance, some form of home improvement, or even the purchase of a new home. Or you might be setting prices of items you're planning to sell online. In those situations, it's always wise to take a step back, examine how you feel, and put off that activity until you're feeling emotionally neutral.

Finally, those of us looking to influence others' decisions should also be aware of the role that mood plays. Of course, it would be both unwise and wrong to attempt to persuade someone who has just been saddened by a piece of information—or even worse, to bring up some topic that will put the other person in a gloomy mood (e.g., "Hey, I heard the bad news about your dog—on an unrelated note, here's the price I can offer for our deal"). Such decisions will often lead to regret and do little to build long-term relationships with others. In fact, by offering to postpone negotiations with someone who has just had a negative emotional experience, you'll strengthen your relationship by making yourself seem noble, caring, and wise, which are three priceless characteristics of anyone who wishes to be more influential.

45

What can make people believe everything they read?

A former Chinese political prisoner once described his experiences as a target of brainwashing:

> You are annihilated, exhausted, you can't control yourself, or remember what you said two minutes before. You feel that all is lost. From that moment the judge is the real master of you. You accept *anything* he says. [emphasis added][88]

To what technique was the former political prisoner referring, and what can this tell us about the factors that allow others to persuade us?

Although the former prisoner was likely the victim of numerous and varied thought-reform tactics, one of the main strategies he was referring to was sleep deprivation. It should come as no surprise that we tend to function better as a whole when we have had a good night's sleep. As we all know from experience, when we're well rested, we're more focused, we feel more alert, and we communicate more eloquently. But work done by social psychologist Daniel Gilbert offers an insight that's less obvious but completely consistent with the experiences of the political prisoner: We may be more susceptible to others' deceptive influence tactics when we are tired. In a series of studies, Gilbert has found evidence supporting the hypothesis that upon hearing someone make a statement, the listener immediately accepts it as true, regardless of whether it's actually true. It is only with mental effort that, a fraction of a second later, the listener recognizes a statement to be false, subsequently rejecting it.

When the stakes are high, people usually have enough cognitive resources and motivation to mentally reject statements that sound false. But when people are tired, they're more likely to be in a heightened state of gullibility because of the diminished cognitive energy and motivation associated with exhaustion. According to Gilbert's findings, the consequence of this diminished energy is that the process of comprehending a message gets cut off before the rejection stage ever has a chance to take place, making people more likely to believe others' weak arguments or downright falsehoods. For example, a manager soliciting bids for a big distribution contract would be less inclined to question a statement made by a potential distributor such as, "Our distribution systems are top-rated globally," when operating on little sleep. Instead, he or she is likely to take this statement at face value.[89]

It's not only sleep deprivation or fatigue that can lead us to become more easily persuaded. Studies also demonstrate that distraction has a similar effect on our susceptibility to influence, even if that distraction is only momentary. For example, research conducted by Barbara Davis and Eric Knowles found that homeowners were twice as likely to purchase Christmas cards from a door-to-door salesperson when the salesperson distracted them by unexpectedly announcing the price in pennies—rather than dollars, which is clearly more typical—before stating, "It's a bargain!" Their studies also show that it wasn't simply a matter of stating the price in pennies that increased the sales rate: The rate of compliance with the request to purchase a pack of cards was higher than a standard appeal only when the price was followed by the persuasive statement, "It's a bargain!" The findings reveal that it's during this instant of momentary distraction that the salesperson can stealthily insert a persuasive assertion under the radar.[90]

In another study conducted by the same research team, people walking around an outdoor bake sale were more likely to purchase a cupcake when the vendors referred to them as "halfcakes" rather than "cupcakes" but only when this was followed by the declaration, "They're delicious!"

What do these studies say about how to avoid succumbing to the factors that make us more easily persuaded? Our first recommendation would be to get more sleep. Of course, we'd all like to get more shut-eye, and we understand that's easier said than done. If you do happen to find yourself particularly distracted or sleep-deprived, however, try to stay away from programs such as infomercials, which often make dubious claims. If you don't, you may end up convinced that you really do need an exercise bike that also pops popcorn while you pedal.

Instead, try to make important decisions that rely on judgments of the truthfulness of others' claims when you feel most awake—for some people, it'll be in the morning, and for others, it'll be later in the day.

Second, if you're charged with a task—let's say, for instance, that it's choosing a new supplier—it's important that you recognize that you're more likely to believe what you read on a prospective supplier's website or formal bid if you're also being distracted, for example, by talking on the phone. Instead, you're likely to make more accurate evaluations of others' statements and will be generally more resistant to deceptive persuasion tactics if you minimize your distractions. You might, for instance, have a personal "decision space" at work or home that's free of distractions and background noise so that you can focus on the task at hand. More practically speaking, to prevent being first duped (by a double-dealing persuader) and then dumped (by your dissatisfied organization), it's a good idea to reduce multitasking when the stakes for these decisions and interactions with others are high.

46

Are trimeth labs boosting your influence?

Bedwetting, dry mouth, and even restless legs. These days, there's seemingly a drug for everything under the sun. You might be surprised to learn, however, that there's a drug called 1, 3, 7-trimethylxanthin that could make you more persuadable if you take it and make you more persuasive if you give it to others. Perhaps even more shocking is the fact that this drug is now widely available through "trimeth labs" that are popping up in neighborhoods everywhere.

The drug, known in the chemistry community as 1, 3, 7-trimethylxanthin, is more commonly known as caffeine, and these "trimeth labs" are more commonly known as coffee shops. Starbucks Corp. alone has over nine thousand locations across thirty-eight countries, although we doubt chairman Howard Schultz ever dreamed that the beverages he'd make available on every street corner and in every shopping mall could be a potential tool of influence and persuasion. We all know that caffeine can make us feel more alert, but can it make us more persuasive?

To test coffee's persuasive prowess, scientist Pearl Martin and her colleagues first asked all of their participants to drink a product resembling orange juice. Like a mischievous teen adding the contents of his flask to the punch bowl at the high-school dance, the researchers spiked the orange drink before serving it to half of their research subjects. But rather than turning the drink into a screwdriver, the researchers instead spiked it with caffeine—approximately the amount that you might find in two cups of espresso.

Shortly after drinking the juice, all the participants read a series of messages containing very good arguments advocating a certain position on a controversial issue. Those who had consumed the caffeinated beverages before reading these arguments were 35 percent more favorably disposed toward that position than were those who drank the unadulterated drink.

Does this mean that you could walk down to the nearest coffee shop on your lunch break and sell the Brooklyn Bridge to any one of the patrons there? Hardly. In a second study, the researchers also tested the effect of caffeine when participants read messages containing weak arguments. The results showed that caffeine has little persuasive power under these circumstances.[91]

Given a choice, then, you should make your presentations when people are most alert—shortly after they've had their morning coffee fix, and never right after lunch. Even if you can't choose the time of day, having coffee or caffeinated tea on hand should make your audience more receptive to your message. But be aware that it usually takes about forty minutes for the full effect of caffeine to kick in, so in a ninety-minute presentation, you may want to stop at the midway point to summarize your best arguments for whatever you've been pitching.

Of course, as the research suggests, this strategy is likely to be effective only if your arguments are genuine, thoughtful, and well reasoned. If they aren't, caffeine is likely to have no effect or, worse still, there's a possibility that a caffeinated audience will be more resistant to your poorly reasoned arguments than a noncaffeinated audience. If that's the case, and you still plan to serve refreshments, we suppose there's always decaf . . .

47

How can technology impede persuasive progress?

Just like any other communications company, U.S. Cellular, a large wireless carrier based in the Midwest, relies almost entirely on technology as the backbone of its business. That's why a policy that the company enacted several years ago seems so ironic, if not completely insane: Over five thousand employees were told that they were no longer allowed to communicate with one another via email on Fridays.

How could that be possible? In an age in which we're all so dependent on electronic transmissions to communicate quickly, effectively, and accurately with our coworkers, banning email is almost like prohibiting the use of calculators in favor of fingers and toes. Why would U.S. Cellular executive vice president Jay Ellison make such a decree? Was it perhaps a nefarious plan concocted by upper management to force their employees to run up personal cell phone bills, thereby increasing profits for the company in the short term?

It turns out that after getting bombarded with more emails every day than he could open, Ellison started to feel that the endless stream of impersonal, electronic communications might actually be hurting teamwork and overall productivity, not improving it. According to an ABCNews.com report, Ellison's memo told employees to "get out to meet your teams face-to-face. Pick up the phone and give someone a call . . . I look forward to not hearing from any of you, but stop by as often as you like." [92]

The news report went on to describe some of the dramatic consequences of the policy change. For example, two coworkers who previously had an email-only relationship were forced to talk to each other by phone. In the course of doing so, they were surprised to learn that they were not in fact across the country from each other, but rather across the hall! This discovery led to face-to-face interactions, which further strengthened their relationship.

The employees were also sure to receive another benefit from the policy shift: increased clarity and understanding of their communications with one another. Research conducted by behavioral scientist Justin Kruger and colleagues shows that miscommunications are much more likely to occur through email than face-to-face or over the phone. They argued that voice inflection and physical gestures—two nonverbal cues that are absent in email communications—typically act as important indicators of the true meaning of the communication when the content of the message is in any way ambiguous. This fact alone is enough to make email communications problematic. But what Kruger and his colleagues argue makes it an even more dangerous problem is that the senders of these messages are almost completely unaware that their messages may be misunderstood. Because the senders have full psychological access to their own intentions when they create their messages, they often assume that the message recipient does as well. Indeed, the researchers found that senders overestimated the degree to which receivers understood the tone of the message (e.g., serious or sarcastic; angry or sad). Remarkably, the pattern of data looks exactly the same regardless of whether participant pairs are close friends or two people who had never interacted before. The fact that written communication can't be fully deciphered even by people who are close to one another suggests that even though you may think that your friends can read you like a book, that's only the case if they're getting you in audiobook format or the made-for-TV version.[93]

So what's a communicator to do about this potential deficiency? Perhaps you could simply use "emoticons," those funny little faces that are intended to convey emotion pictorially (e.g., ":-("). However, as evidenced by this graphically challenged example, emoticons can also blend into the rest of the message or be unclear in other ways, resulting in additional confusion. How about eliminating emails entirely, choosing to communicate only through phone or face-to-face interactions? Maybe that might work once a week, as at U.S. Cellular, but we don't always have the time or ability to engage in such interactions. According to the findings of an additional study, Kruger and his colleagues suggest that simply having senders pause for a moment to reflect on how their email might be perceived differently than intended can drastically reduce this problem.

Although it no doubt took some time to get accustomed to, the consensus at U.S. Cellular today is that the no email Fridays policy has been a resounding success and serves as an important reminder about the role that personal interactions with others plays in strengthening our relationships with them. But the case of U.S. Cellular dealt primarily with the consequences of electronic interactions for general workplace relationships and communication. What about e-influence?

For example, how is a process like negotiation affected by whether it takes place online or face-to-face? Gone are the days when negotiations were conducted exclusively in person. Today, negotiations are being conducted online with increasing frequency, with the stakes ranging from the terms of a multibillion-dollar contract to the pizza toppings for next month's office party.

Although the internet has often been referred to as the information superhighway, might the lack of personal contact between negotiating parties have the potential to act more like a roadblock than a route to successful outcomes? Research conducted by social scientist Michael Morris and colleagues made this argument. In one experiment, MBA students negotiated with one another either face-to-face or via email. When all was said and done, those who negotiated through email exchanged far less of the kind of personal information that typically helps people establish better rapport.[94]

Realizing that the lack of rapport created through e-negotiation could lead to poorer outcomes for all parties, researcher Don Moore and his colleagues thought they might have a pretty simple fix to this potentially not-so-simple problem: What if, before the negotiation, the negotiators engaged in some form of mutual self-disclosure? In other words, they could get to know a little bit about one another's background in addition to e-schmoozing for a few minutes on topics unrelated to the negotiation before the negotiation takes place. To test this idea, the researchers paired up students enrolled at two elite U.S. business schools and had them negotiate a deal via email. Whereas half were simply given the instructions to negotiate, the other half were provided with a photograph of the negotiating partner, some brief biographical information about the partner (e.g., undergraduate alma mater, interests), and instructions to spend some time before the negotiation getting to know one another through email.

When the participants were given no additional information, 29 percent of the pairs came to an impasse, failing to agree on a deal. However, only 6 percent of the more "personalized" pairs came to an impasse. Using another measure of negotiation success, the researchers also found that when the pairs involved in the experiment were able to come to a mutually agreeable negotiated solution, the joint outcome of the negotiated settlement— the sum of what each participant walked away with—was 18 percent higher in the personalized groups as compared to the depersonalized groups.[95] So, by taking the time to disclose something personal about yourself and to learn something personal about your online counterpart, you'll likely be able to increase the size of the pie for you both to share. The bottom line is this: It's okay to use a computer to persuade. Just don't act like one when you do.

48

How do you get to yes in
any language?

Hai. Hao. Da. Ja. Sí. Oui. People from around the
globe say yes in very different ways, but does
that mean that the persuasion strategies we use to get
them to say it should also differ depending on the message recipient's cultural background? Or is a one-size-fits-
all approach likely to be equally effective regardless of a
person's country of origin? Although the fundamental
principles of social influence and many of the strategies
we discuss throughout this book are powerful persuaders in all cultures, recent research suggests that there are
some subtle differences in how to tailor your tactics and
your messages based on the cultural background of the
person you're trying to persuade. In essence, these differences result from the variation in the cultural norms and
traditions of diverse societies, which leads the people of
these different societies to place greater weight on some
aspects of a persuasive message than on others. This
means that successful organizations looking to transfer
their practices, policies, and organizational structures
from one cultural setting to another need to pay careful

attention to how social influence differs in the two cultures—or risk turning what may be a well-oiled machine in one society into a gunk-filled clunker in the next.

Social influence researchers have focused much of their attention on how one particular dimension, known as individualism-collectivism, affects the persuasion process. In brief, individualism is an orientation that assigns highest priority to the preferences and rights of the individual. Collectivism, on the other hand, is an orientation that assigns highest priority to the preferences and rights of the group. Although it's an oversimplification, one might say that in individualistic cultures, it's more about *me,* whereas in collectivistic cultures, it's more about *we.* People in countries like the United States, the United Kingdom, and others in Western Europe tend to be more individualistic. In contrast, many other countries around the globe, including those that are now burgeoning areas for international business partnerships—those in Asia, South America, Africa, and Eastern Europe—are more collectivistic.

Researchers Sang-Pil Han and Sharon Shavitt set out to examine the implications of these different cultural orientations on persuasion in a marketing context. Their prediction was that in collectivistic cultures, advertisements that focus consumers on the product's benefits to one's group members (e.g., friends, family, or coworkers) would be more persuasive than advertisements that focus consumers solely on the product's benefits for the consumer him- or herself. They also thought that this would be especially likely for products that are typically shared with others, such as air conditioners or toothpaste.

Han and Shavitt first looked for evidence to support their ideas. They picked two magazines in the United States and two magazines in South Korea, making sure that they matched the magazines in the two countries on overall popularity and genre. They then randomly selected advertisements from those magazines and had trained native and bilingual speakers evaluate the ads for the extent to which the ads focused on the benefit of the product to the reader him- or herself or on the benefit of the product to the reader's group. The researchers found that U.S. ads were indeed more likely than South Korean ads to highlight how the product's benefits were conferred on the individual rather than on the group, especially for products that are shared with others. Whereas the U.S. advertisements tended to appeal to the reader's individuality (e.g., "The art of being unique"), motivation for self-improvement (e.g., "You, only better"), and personal goals (e.g., "With this new look I'm ready for my new role"), the South Korean advertisements tended to appeal to the reader's sense of responsibility to the group (e.g., "A more exhilarating way to provide for your family"), motivation to enhance the group (e.g., "The dream of prosperity for all of us"), and consideration of the group's opinions (e.g., "Our family agrees with the selection of home-furnishings").

After confirming that the persuasive messages embedded in these advertisements targeted different consumer motivations based on the cultural orientation of the society, the researchers wanted to answer a more psychologically important question: Are collectivistic- and individualistic-oriented messages actually more persuasive in their respective cultures? After all, as we discussed in the Introduction, that marketers think certain types of messages will be most effective doesn't simply make it so.

To answer this question, Han and Shavitt created two versions of advertisements for a variety of products—one version was more individualistic-oriented and the other was more collectivistic-oriented. For example, the individualistic version of an ad for a brand of chewing gum stated, "Treat yourself to a breath-freshening experience." Notice that this message is focused on the breath-freshening benefits solely to the consumer. But as we all know from experience, the state of a person's breath isn't solely a personal issue; it can affect those around that person as well. Understandably, then, the more collectivistic version of this ad stated, "Share the breath-freshening experience." Of course, the ads were written in English for the U.S. participants and in Korean for the South Korean participants. The results revealed that South Korean participants were more persuaded by the collectivistic than the individualistic ad, and the reverse was true for U.S. participants. And, consistent with the earlier study, this effect was especially powerful with products that people tend to share with others.[96]

These findings should also give pause to any marketer considering blanketing various countries with a one-strategy-fits-all marketing campaign. Instead, such campaigns should be tailored to fit the particular cultural orientation of the societies in which they take place. The breath of an entire nation may depend on it.

49

How can you avoid driving your cross-cultural influence into the rough?

everal years ago, legendary U.S. golfer Jack Nicklaus suffered a nearly unbearable tragedy, witnessing the heartbreaking death of his young grandson. Several days later, Nicklaus made it clear in an interview that his chances of playing in one of golf's most prestigious events, the Masters, were "between slim and none." Yet, to the surprise of many, he also announced that he would play in two other golf outings in the near future. What powerful factor could convince a grieving man to participate in these events after being stricken by such tragedy?

It turns out that Nicklaus had made prior promises to play in each event before his grandson passed away. As the golfer put it, "You make commitments, and you've got to do them." [97] As we discussed earlier, the motivation to be consistent with one's commitments can be quite powerful in influencing a person's actions. But does it motivate with the same force equally across cultures?

All else being equal, would someone from a different cultural background feel just as bound by his or her previous actions and commitments at a time of family tragedy?

To help get a better understanding of the answer to this question, let's consider an experiment that one of us conducted with lead researcher Petia Petrova. In that experiment, students who were native to the United States (generally more individualistic) and students who were Asian international students (generally more collectivistic) received an email that asked them to complete an online survey. A month after receiving the first request, each participant received a second email requesting their participation in another online survey related to the first project, which they were told would take about double the amount of time to complete as the original survey.

When we looked at the compliance rates for the first request, we found that U.S. students were actually slightly less likely to comply with the initial request than were their Asian counterparts. Yet, of the participants who did comply with the initial request, the U.S. participants were actually more likely to comply with the second request (around 22 percent) than the Asian participants (around 10 percent). Put another way, we found that compliance with the initial request had a far greater influence on subsequent compliance among U.S. participants than among Asian participants.[98]

Why did this occur? Perhaps some additional research that one of us conducted might shed more light on this perplexing question. Along with several colleagues, we conducted a study in which we found that when we asked American students to participate without pay in a marketing survey, they were more influenced by their own history of agreement to such requests—in other words, to their prior commitments—than by their peers' history of agreement. But in Poland, a more collectivistic-oriented country, just the opposite occurred. In Poland, what a student's peer group had previously done was a more powerful motivator of current compliance than what the student him- or herself had previously done.[99]

These findings are primarily due to cultural differences in individualism and collectivism. Because people from individualistic cultures tend to give greater weight to their own personal experiences, consistency with one's previous experiences is often a more potent motivator of people from countries in North America or Western Europe. And because people from collectivistic cultures tend to give greater weight to the experiences of close others, the behavior of close others is often a more powerful motivator of people from countries in Asia, Eastern Europe, South America, and Africa. What this means is that when asking an American, Canadian, or Briton for a favor, you are likely to be more successful if you point out that it fits with what that person has done before. But when asking a favor of people from more collectivistic countries, the research suggests that you will be more successful if you point out that it fits with what that person's peer group has done before.

To take a specific example, suppose you worked for a company that has been doing business successfully with a firm in Eastern Europe for two years. During that time, you have often had to ask your European partners for the favor of providing updated marketing information. Your main contact there, Slawek, and his coworkers have usually gone out of their way to help you. Suppose further that you need updated information once more and that in a phone conversation you make your request as follows: "Slawek, you have been so helpful in the past that I'm hoping you can provide us with updated information again." In so doing, you will have made a mistake. The results of these studies suggest that you would have better success if you had said, "Slawek, you *and* your coworkers have been so helpful in the past that I'm hoping that you can provide us with updated information again." It's an easy mistake for a North American, British, or Western European person to make because those individuals assume that everyone prefers to operate according to the principle of personal consistency—the tendency to decide what's right to do in a situation based on what one has previously done there. But, as these studies demonstrated, in many collectivistic countries, personal consistency with one's prior actions is outweighed by the principle of social proof—the tendency to decide what's right to do in a situation based on what one's group has previously done.

50

When does letting the call go to voicemail cause a hang-up in your influence?

If you're like us, it happens to you all the time. You should probably take the call, but for one reason or another, you don't. You might be eating lunch. Perhaps you're busy surfing the web for the latest sports scores. Or maybe you just like the way the cell phone feels when it vibrates in your pocket. Regardless of the reason, the negative impact is usually minimal: The caller typically leaves a message, which you can return at a time that's more convenient. But why might this common routine have more dire consequences if the caller is from a collectivistic rather than an individualistic culture?

People from collectivistic and individualistic cultures tend to differ in the relative weight they give to two central functions of communication. In short, one function of communication is informational: When we communicate, we convey information to others. A second, less obvious function of communication is relational: When we communicate, we help build and maintain relationships with others. Although both functions are clearly important to people in all cultures, social psychologists Yuri Miyamoto and Norbert Schwarz argued that individualistic cultures place a greater emphasis on the informational function of communication, whereas collectivistic cultures place a greater emphasis on the relational function.

Although this cultural difference has implications for a variety of communication-related issues, Miyamoto and Schwarz examined one aspect of communication that permeates our daily lives both at home and in the workplace—leaving phone messages for others. The researchers suspected that because people from Japan tend to be collectivistic and therefore more focused on forming and maintaining relationships with others, Japanese people would have a harder time making a somewhat complex request on an answering machine. They reasoned that if Japanese people care more about how their communications affect their relationship with message recipients than American people, conveying a message in which they receive no feedback about how the message is being received should cause them to experience more mental fatigue. To test this, Miyamoto and Schwarz had American and Japanese participants leave a somewhat detailed request for help on an answering machine using their native languages. Whereas American participants cut right to the heart of the information, Japanese participants took longer to leave their messages, seeming to be more concerned about how their message would affect their relationship with the recipient.

The researchers also surveyed Japanese and American participants about their experiences with answering machines. Whereas Americans reported hanging up when reaching an answering machine about half the time, Japanese people reported hanging up an astounding 85 percent of the time. And, consistent with the researchers' explanation for the results of the previous study, when asked what they disliked most about answering machines, the Japanese respondents were more likely to cite relational reasons (e.g., "It is hard to sound personal on the answering machine") than were Americans, whereas the cultural pattern was reversed for informational reasons (e.g., "People sometimes don't check it").[100]

What do these findings say about influencing others within and outside the workplace? As we discussed in previous chapters, relationships are a key component to the persuasion process—but this is especially true with people from countries with collectivistic orientations. When leaving messages for others, it can be tempting, especially to people from individualistic cultures, to focus entirely on efficiently and succinctly conveying a piece of information while ignoring one's relationship with the message receiver. These results suggest that, when dealing with people from collectivistic cultures, it is particularly important to attend to aspects of the relationship that the two of you share.[101]

The same should apply for conversations as well. In fact, based on some prior research showing how Japanese listeners tend to provide more feedback (e.g., "I see," "Yes") than their American counterparts during conversations, Miyamoto and Schwarz suggest that when a Japanese person talks to an American, it's almost as if that person is talking to an answering machine. This idea fits with an additional survey finding that Japanese participants were more likely to say that they disliked answering machines because "it is hard to speak because there are no responses." These findings also suggest that we should be especially vigilant about providing such feedback with people from collectivistic cultures, letting them know that we're attending to the relationship that we share with them as well as to the information they're trying to convey.[102]

The results also serve as a warning that "letting the call go to voicemail" can be a potentially treacherous decision, especially when the caller is from a collectivistic culture. If you think that the worst that can happen is that you get yourself into a simple game of "phone tag," you might soon find that a simple sound–*click*–informs you that it's now become a single-player game.

Epilogue

hroughout this book, we've described many social influence strategies that we've referred to as tools for your persuasion toolbox. And that's exactly how they should be used—as constructive tools that help build authentic relationships with others, highlight the genuine strengths of one's message, initiative, or product, and ultimately create outcomes that are in the best interest of all parties. However, when these tools are instead used unethically as weapons of influence—for example, by dishonestly or artificially importing the principles of social influence into situations in which they don't naturally exist—any short-term gains will almost invariably be followed by long-term losses. In other words, although the dishonest use of persuasion strategies may occasionally work in the short run—perhaps someone could be persuaded with a bad set of arguments or could be tricked into buying a defective product—the long-term consequences to one's reputation are dire when this dishonesty eventually is discovered.

It's not simply the dishonest use of persuasion tools that people would be wise to avoid; there are also inherent dangers in trying to exploit the applications of some of the tools that we've described. For example, in the spring of 2000, the United Kingdom found itself in the midst of a serious crisis. Businesses up and down the country were crying out in desperation; schools were deserted; shops were struggling to find customers; and public services were at risk of a meltdown. The reason for the crisis? There was no fuel. Actually, that last statement is only partially true. There was plenty of fuel; it was just that stations had no supplies due to the blockading of a number of oil refineries by protesters who were upset with how much they had to pay at the pump.

The impact of the shortage quickly took effect. In every city, town, and village, tens of thousands of motorists quickly formed lines outside fuel stations to fill up with much-needed supplies. As the shortage began to take a deeper effect, the behavior of the motorists also changed. Local and national newspapers, radio stations, and TV channels ran stories describing how car owners would join one queue to fill their tanks with fuel only to drive a few miles down the road and join another one to top off their tanks again. Other drivers slept overnight in their cars outside fuel stations, hoping they might be the lucky recipients of one of the rare shipments of fuel that did get through the blockades. This is the power of scarcity in action.

At the height of the crisis, there was a gas station owner who had reportedly received a supply of much-needed fuel. In fact, he was the only owner for many miles around with supplies of fuel, and the news quickly spread. Recognizing the unique position in which he found himself, and seeing the lengthy line forming outside his business, none of us would be surprised to learn that this enterprising businessman took advantage of his fortunate situation by adding a premium to the price of his fuel. But instead of adding a small amount, he increased his prices tenfold, which amounted to the equivalent of over forty dollars per gallon!

Did the disgruntled but still fuel-hungry motorists refuse en masse to pay such extortionate prices? Hardly. Although they were angry, they still lined up in droves to get whatever fuel they could from the station. In just a matter of hours, the last drop of fuel had been drained from the station's tank, and the owner made a profit in one single day that would have normally taken him two weeks to attain.

But what happened to his business two weeks later, after the crisis had ended? In a word, it was disastrous. By exploiting the scarcity of the fuel and forcing desperate drivers to pay ridiculously inflated prices, he profited in the short term but completely lost out in the long run. People simply boycotted his business. Some went further, making it their goal to inform their friends, neighbors, and coworkers about the owner's actions. His business lost nearly every customer it had, and within a very short time, his damaged reputation forced him to close. This is completely consistent with an abundance of research showing that those who behave in an untrustworthy matter can do little to regain the public's trust.[103]

If the owner had considered the set of powerful social influence tools available to him in his persuasion toolbox, certainly there were better choices available– choices that could have led to far greater profits in the long term. For one, he could have ensured that his fuel supplies went primarily to his local or regular customers, making a point of informing them that the reason he was doing so was that he valued their loyalty. Or, he could have put up a sign saying that he refused to gouge needy motorists in a time of crisis; acting against his own (short-term) self-interest in this way certainly would have made him appear more likable, generous, and trustworthy in the motorists' eyes, a move that surely would have paid big dividends in the future. Even if he had done nothing but keep the prices reasonable, customers would have likely been more than happy to buy some extras from the shop just because they felt grateful that he didn't take advantage of them under those trying circumstances.

In a way, though, the gas station owner's actions are somewhat understandable. In the same way that many of the people we wish to influence are often forced to make decisions quickly by the fast-paced world around them, the same is true for us as the persuaders. Often the first influence strategy that comes to mind will not be the most ethical—or the wisest, as was demonstrated by the outcome of the owner's actions. But by taking the extra effort to consider all of the available options—and by now, you should have a toolbox full of them—you can move people toward your perspective, product, or initiative in a way that's genuine, honest, and long-lasting. And at the same time, as ethical persuaders, we can take comfort in knowing that those who do choose to wield social influence as a destructive weapon, rather than a constructive tool, will inevitably end up pointing that weapon at themselves and shooting themselves in the foot.

Appendix:
Feedback from Those Who've Used These Methods

I n this book, we've attempted to discuss a number of insights into how the influence process works from a scientific perspective. We have been vigilant in providing only the influence strategies that have been shown, through rigorously controlled studies and research, to be effective. We deliberately haven't based our recommendations on our own hunches or anecdotes. Instead, we've relied entirely on the significant body of research from the study of social influence and persuasion. Accordingly, you can be confident that your own attempts to influence and persuade others no longer need be based solely on your own intuition and experience. You now also have science on your side.

We're frequently contacted by people who report to us their experiences in using the science of persuasion, often in response to reading one of our books, attending one of our seminars or conference keynote talks, or receiving our free monthly online *Inside Influence Report*. These people come from many different types of work settings. Some work for multinational corporations, others in government or education, others are self-employed, and yet others are people who simply want to satisfy their curiosity regarding what science tells us about how to be persuasive. All of them have one thing in common: They shared with us a story about how they ethically employed one or more of these scientific insights in a way that has helped them to become more persuasive. We've included below a selection of readers' reports that relate to methods introduced in this book, arranged by chapter topic.

2. What shifts the bandwagon effect into another gear?

Tim Batchelor, Training Manager, Surrey

While in the role of head of training at a major pharmaceutical company, I had the responsibility of launching a new presentation skills program to our four hundred U.K. sales staff. While we knew that the program was very innovative, we also knew that not everyone would think the same as us about the initiative. A lot of the staff had been in the organization for some years and probably thought they had seen it all before. Based on the idea that people follow the lead of lots of others like them, in the first couple of workshops we asked people to write down one thing they genuinely liked about the workshop. We took that good feedback and printed it on large posters, which we displayed on the walls at future events. In fact, before we started any training we asked delegates to review the posters and see what their colleagues were saying about the program. I was a little skeptical at first about whether such a simple thing would work, but the impact was incredible. By the end of the program rollout we had collected more than two hundred emails from people who had attended (an unprecedented number). What was interesting was that this catalog of testimonials also helped me to influence senior managers to support future projects I was leading. After all, it wasn't just me telling them how great the training department was. I now had the written testimonials of two hundred staff saying so as well.

Authors' note: What's especially wise about Tim's use of social proof is that, by simply asking the first group of program participants to write down their testimonials, he was able to use the same testimonials both to convince others of the value of the program and to make the testifiers' already positive feelings toward the program even stronger.

5. When does offering people more make them want less?

John Fisher, Preston, United Kingdom

My wife had her own business making and selling children's clothes. When she first started up, she had only a few styles and fabric patterns to offer her customers. As her business started to grow and she attracted new customers, she decided to expand the range she offered. We consistently found that the more choices people had, the less they bought. While, like most people, we would consider more choices to be a good thing, my wife found that having lots of options for her customers often meant they did less business with her.

Authors' note: With all the choices that parents have to make—what to feed their children, where and when to enroll them in school, how to encourage them and discipline them, to name a few—it's perhaps no surprise that having an abundance of choices for their children's clothes might just be overwhelming. John's report provides an important lesson: Downsize the number of options we offer to others when they must face a profusion of choices in other areas of their lives.

13. Do favors behave like bread or like wine?

Dan Norris, Director of Training, Holt Development Services, San Antonio, Texas

Giveaways are a hallmark of the sports franchise world. Be it bobble heads, T-shirts, or free seats, many teams use them to lure fans to games. The owner of our company owns several sports teams, including a minor-league hockey club. After a period of low ticket sales, we had to report to our season ticket holders that we had to cut back our promotional giveaways. We scheduled several focus groups, and the first group reacted very negatively to the news. They viewed the giveaways almost as an expectation rather than a gift. We inadvertently had them focus on the possibility that the very things they had come to expect would be cut back. The meetings quickly spiraled downward, and many friends went home angry.

Afterward, we met to discuss a different strategy, and thought about how we could be more effective by applying the principle of reciprocity. At our next focus group meeting, we started off by asking the fans to name the different giveaways we'd offered over the years. They began to call out answers like jerseys, extra tickets, and autographed hockey sticks. We followed up their answers by saying, "We are happy we have been able to provide those gifts to you in the past, and would like to continue to do so in the future. However, our ticket sales are falling and that will make that difficult. What can we do together to help bring in more fans to the games?" The reaction couldn't have been more different from that of the first group. The fans began collaborating on how they could get more of their friends and family members to attend the games, and some even remarked, "It's the least we can do after all of the great things you've done for us."

Authors' note: This story demonstrates another way in which recipients of gifts and favors become less grateful over time: If they receive gifts often enough, they begin to see them as a right rather than as a generous gesture. The solution Dan's group generated for getting the fans to reclassify the promotional items as gifts and to remind themselves of all that the hockey club had done for them in the past was both ethical and effective.

14. How can one small step help your influence take a giant leap?

Nick Pope, Director of Sales Force Training (Europe, Middle East, Africa), Bausch and Lomb

One way we develop relationships with customers is to invite them to educational presentations and meetings. These days, our customers are bombarded with requests to attend meetings and study days that are sponsored by different companies. It's no wonder that sometimes many of those who initially say they will attend an event do not actually turn up. This can have a significant impact on our business. Using the principle of commitment and consistency, before we invite any customers to an important meeting, we ask them (a) to register their interest in a particular subject and then (b) to create a few questions that they would like answered on the topic.

When they receive their invite we make it clear that some of these questions will be answered by our guest speaker and expert on the topic. The expectation that their question (which they have already committed to asking) could be asked in an open forum has seen participant levels dramatically increase since using this principle.

Authors' note: Although the principle of commitment and consistency seems simple, we often must ask ourselves the question, "Committed to *what*?" Or "Consistent with *what*?" Here, Nick and his team give themselves a head start in this effort by focusing on the questions that each of the potential attendees already finds personally most interesting.

16. How can a simple question drastically increase support for you and your ideas?

Kathy Fragnoli, The Resolution Group, Dallas and San Diego

I am an attorney who left the practice of law thirteen years ago to become a full-time mediator. My job is to meet with parties who are involved in litigation and help them settle their disputes. Most are represented by lawyers. A typical mediation starts with all of the parties in one room. Each is asked to provide a statement of their case. After opening statements, I escort each side to their respective rooms, and I go back and forth between them in an effort to persuade each litigant that the position he or she took early in the morning needs to shift for the case to settle. I often provide private input on the strengths and weaknesses of each case to facilitate movement. Before I read about the psychology of persuasion, I would allow the parties to state their monetary demands in the opening session for the other party to hear. Once I understood the principle of consistency, however, I began requesting that each side hold off on their monetary demands or offers until I met with them privately. My settlement rate increased dramatically when I realized that the public commitment to a number was hindering the effort to compromise. I quickly realized that the more people in the room who heard the opening demands, the harder it was to move them away from their positions!

Authors' note: Kathy's report very aptly shows the negative side of public commitments. Because such commitments lead people to defend their original stands, we should avoid beginning a meeting by asking individuals to state their positions regarding the best way to handle the issue at hand. Instead, all of the available options should be discussed at the start of a meeting; then, after everyone has had an opportunity to consider all the evidence, people will have an opportunity to publicly support a particular course of action. That will increase the chances that any conflicts throughout the meeting will involve attempts to find the optimal solution rather than attempts to save face.

22. How can we show off what we know without being labeled a show-off?

Dil Sidhu, Acting Assistant Chief Executive,
London Borough of Lambeth

When I moved to this office, the borough had major problems with operations, leadership, and managing change and was undergoing a major recovery program. By using the principle of authority (which maintains that people rely on those with superior knowledge or wisdom for guidance on how to respond), I found useful ways of ensuring that the government monitoring and advisory panel was accepting of the type and speed of change being achieved. I ensured that the credentials of the people brought in to work on the turnaround were well publicized along with the names of other organizations where they had been instrumental in improving performance. A small thing, but it elicited a huge attitude change from the advisory panel and allowed us the freedom to get on with the job of recovery.

Authors' note: Note how little cost there was to the changes that Dil made. All the information about the people being brought in was already there for dissemination; it was just a matter of communicating it to the audience before any influence was attempted.

33. When is a loser a winner?

*Brian F. Ahearn, State Auto Insurance Companies,
Columbus, Ohio*

One of my responsibilities is to help recruit new independent agencies to represent our company. In our effort to do this, we sent marketing materials to prospective agencies so they could learn more about us. While we hope most agents read our communications, seldom did we receive any direct replies. After learning about the principle of scarcity we realized we were missing out on an opportunity that had been right in front of us all along! We don't do business in every state, and each year we set a modest goal for appointing new agents in our operating areas. We never thought to incorporate those facts, or our current progress, into the communications we were sending. Understanding how scarcity can move people to action, we began to include something like this near the end of our communications: "Each year we have a goal of selecting just a few new agencies to partner with us. For 2006 that number was set at only forty-two agencies across our twenty-eight operating states, and so far we've appointed more than thirty-five. It's our sincere hope that your agency will be one of those remaining agencies we appoint before year end." The difference was noticeable immediately! Within days we began to receive inquiries. No extra cost, no new marketing campaigns, no product or system changes needed. The only change was adding three more sentences that contain true statements.

Authors' note: Brian's report is a perfect example of the benefits of thinking about what his organization had to offer that was genuinely scarce, and honestly describing it.

34. What can you gain from loss?

Christy Farnbauch, Hilliard City Schools, Hilliard, Ohio

I had the opportunity to put some of the principles to the test during a school bond campaign. I work for the ninth-largest school district in Ohio and we tried, unsuccessfully, three times to pass a bond levy that would provide funding for a third high school and fourteenth elementary school. During the last campaign (February through May 2006), I suggested that we try some new tactics based on the science of persuasion. We chose a campaign theme worded in the negative: "Our Kids Can't Wait." In the past, campaign themes had always been positive (for example, "Unite for Kids," "Building Tomorrow Today"). We were trying to communicate a sense of limited time to do the right thing and to touch on loss aversion. The implication was that our kids (and the community) would lose if we didn't act now. We developed three clear messages, based on community research, and clearly articulated those messages over and over (a proven political strategy). We also built a social network of more than ten thousand voters by using a Get Out the Vote strategy called "Mine + 9." Through a phone survey, the most likely supportive voters were identified, and one thousand volunteers were asked to choose nine names of friends or colleagues to call and follow up with over a three-week period before the election.

The volunteers were well informed. The potential voters were asked to make a commitment to voting on the school issue and were simultaneously held accountable by a friend or colleague. They received reminders about the election right up until the polls closed on Election Day. We also created campaign postcards and other communications that were tailored to specific areas throughout the district. Again, a first.

While I can't scientifically prove that any of these strategies helped us win the election, we did pass the issue with a wide margin. I believe that these tactics were invaluable to our success, and we will use them again for future campaigns.

Authors' note: Christy and her team's use of commitment/consistency along with the loss language is but one example of how combining different influence strategies can have an additive effect on success.

We would be delighted to hear from readers of this book who would like to submit an example of their own use of ethical influence for possible inclusion either in future editions of this book or in new books. Please send them to the relevant contact below or submit them via our websites. Additionally, for more information about Influence At Work, our books, conference talks, training, and consultancy services, please contact the relevant addresses on the following page.

In the United States, Canada, and Rest of the World

Influence At Work
The Broadmor Place
2248 South Forest Avenue
Tempe, AZ 85252
United States of America
+1 (0) 480 967 6070
info@influenceatwork.com
www.influenceatwork.com

In the United Kingdom and Europe

Influence At Work (UK)
Dixies Barn D, High Street
Ashwell
Hertfordshire SG7 5NT
United Kingdom
+44 (0) 870 787 4747
info@influenceatwork.co.uk
www.influenceatwork.co.uk

You can sign up and receive our free monthly *Inside Influence Report* by visiting www.influenceatwork.com or www.influenceatwork.co.uk

Notes

Introduction

1. The full reference for Robert Cialdini's book is: Cialdini, R.B. (2001). *Influence: Science and Practice* (4th ed.). Boston: Allyn & Bacon.

1. How can inconveniencing your audience increase your persuasiveness?

2. The staring-upward study can be found in: Milgram, S., Bickman, L., and Berkowitz, L. (1969). Note on the drawing power of crowds of different size. *Journal of Personality & Social Psychology,* 13:79–82.

3. For more on people's frequent inability to correctly report the factors that influence their behavior, see: Nisbett, R., and Wilson, T. (1977). Telling more than we can know: Verbal reports on mental processes. *Psychological Review,* 84:231–59.

4. The hotel study data can be found in: Goldstein, N. J., Cialdini, R. B., and Griskevicius, V. (forthcoming). A room with a viewpoint: Using social norms to motivate environmental conservation in hotels. *Journal of Cosnumr Research.*

5. For those interested in learning more about why there's good reason to follow crowds, see: Surowiecki, J. (2005). *The Wisdom of Crowds.* New York: Doubleday.

2. What shifts the bandwagon effect into another gear?

6. The hotel study data reported in this chapter are from the same hotel study described in the previous chapter.

7. For a set of experiments showing how we automatically associate certain behaviors with specific environments and situations, see: Aarts, H., and Dijksterhuis, A. (2003). The silence of the library: environment, situational norm, and social behavior. *Journal of Personality and Social Psychology.* 84:18–28.

3. What common mistake causes messages to self-destruct?

8. These two public service announcements can be viewed on the Keep America Beautiful Organization's website at: http://www.kab.org/media.asp?id=246&rid=250.

9. The information about the Women's Voices, Women Vote campaign can be found in: Gerber, A. S., and Rogers, T. (forthcoming). The effect of descriptive social norms on voter turnout: The importance of accentuating the positive. *The Journal of Politics.* This paper also describes how positively and negatively framed descriptive norms in get-out-the-vote campaigns produce very different responses.

10. Some of the Petrified Forest data were published in: Cialdini, R. B. (2003). Crafting normative messages to protect the environment. *Current Directions in Psychological Science,* 12:105-9. The PSA data were published there as well.

11. For more on the Petrified Forest studies, see: Cialdini, R. B., Demaine, L. J., Sagarin, B. J., Barrett, D. W., Rhoads, K., and Winter, P. L. (2006). Managing social norms for persuasive impact. *Social Influence,* 1:3-15.

12. For more on this topic, see: Goldstein, N. J., and Cialdini, R. B. (2007). Using social norms as a lever of social influence. In Pratkanis, A. (ed.), *The Science of Social Influence: Advances and Future Progress* (167-91). Philadelphia, PA: Psychology Press.

4. When persuasion might backfire, how do you avoid the magnetic middle?

13. The household energy conservation study can be found in: Schultz, P. W., Nolan, J. M., Cialdini, R. B., Goldstein, N. J., and Griskevicius, V. (2007). The constructive, destructive, and reconstructive power of social norms. *Psychological Science,* 18:429-34.

5. When does offering people more make them want less?

14. The retirement fund analysis can be found in: Iyengar, S. S., Huberman, G., and Jiang, W. (2004). How much choice is too much?: Contributions to 401(k) retirement plans. In Mitchell, O., and Utkus, S. (eds.), *Pension Design and Structure: New Lessons from Behavioral Finance* (83-96). Oxford University Press.

15. The jam choice study can be found in: Iyengar, S. S., and Lepper, M. R. (2000). When choice is demotivating: Can one desire too much of a good thing? *Journal of Personality and Social Psychology,* 79:995-1006.

16. For more on companies' decisions to reduce the number of

alternatives they offer, see: Osnos, E. (1997, September 27). Too many choices? Firms cut back on new products. *Philadelphia Inquirer*, D1, D7.

17. For those interested in learning more about why offering more choices can have a paralyzing or destructive effect on others, see: Schwartz, B. (2004). *The Paradox of Choice*. New York: Ecco.

6. When does a bonus become an onus?

18. The bonus gift boomeranging study can be found in: Raghubir, P. (2004). Free gift with purchase: Promoting or discounting the brand? *Journal of Consumer Psychology*, 14:181–86.

7. How can a new superior product mean more sales of an inferior one?

19. Both the bread-maker example and the research presented in this chapter can be found in: Simonson, I. (1993). Get closer to your customers by understanding how they make choices. *California Management Review*, 35:68–84.

8. Does fear persuade or does it paralyze?

20. The public health study can be found in: Leventhal, H., Singer, R., and Jones, S. (1965). Effects of fear and specificity of recommendation upon attitudes and behavior. *Journal of Personality and Social Psychology*, 2:20–29. Many other studies show similar effects, including, for example: Rogers, R. W., and Mewborn, C. R. (1976). Fear appeals and attitude change: Effects of a threat's noxiousness, probability of occurrence and the efficacy of coping responses. *Journal of Personality and Social Psychology*, 34:54–61.

9. What can chess teach us about making persuasive moves?

21. The news article detailing the reaction in Iceland to Bobby Fischer can be found in: Smith-Spark, L. (2005, March 23). Fisher "put Iceland on the map." Retrieved from http://news.bbc.co.uk/2/hi/europe/4102367.stm.

22. The Regan Coke can study can be found in: Regan, D. T. (1971). Effects of a favor and liking on compliance. *Journal of Experimental Social Psychology*, 7:627–39.

10. What office item can make your influence stick?

23. The Post-it Note research can be found in: Garner, R. (2005). Post-It® Note persuasion: a sticky influence. *Journal of Consumer Psychology*, 15:230–37.

11. Why should restaurants ditch their baskets of mints?

24. The tipping study can be found in: Strohmetz, D. B., Rind, B., Fisher, R., and Lynn, M. (2002). Sweetening the till: the use of candy to increase restaurant tipping. *Journal of Applied Social Psychology,* 32: 300–309.

12. What's the pull of having no strings attached?

25. These hotel study data are from a manuscript currently being prepared to undergo the peer review process: Goldstein, N. J., Cialdini, R. B., and Griskevicius, V. (2008). Maximizing motivation to cooperate toward the fulfillment of a shared goal: Initiation is everything.

13. Do favors behave like bread or like wine?

26. The study examining the effect of time on favor value can be found in: Flynn, F. J. (2003). What have you done for me lately? Temporal adjustments to favor evaluations. *Organizational Behavior and Human Decision Processes,* 91:38–50.

14. How can one small step help your influence take a giant leap?

27. Both the ugly billboard study and the home invasion study can be found in: Freedman, J. L., and Fraser, S. C. (1966). Compliance without pressure: The foot-in-the-door technique. *Journal of Personality and Social Psychology,* 4:195–203.

28. The sales expert advice can be found in: Green, F. (1965). The "foot-in-the-door" technique, *American Salesman,* 10, 14-16.

15. How can you become a Jedi master of persuasion?

29. The labeling technique study involving voting can be found in: Tybout, A. M., and Yalch, R. F. (1980). The effect of experience: A matter of salience? *Journal of Consumer Research,* 6:406–13.

30. The labeling technique study with children can be found in: Cialdini, R. B., Eisenberg, N., Green, B.L., Rhoads, K., and Bator, R. (1998). Undermining the undermining effect of reward on sustained interest: When unnecessary conditions are sufficient. *Journal of Applied Social Psychology,* 28:249–63.

16. How can a simple question drastically increase support for you and your ideas?

31. The voting study can be found in: Greenwald, A. G., Carnot, C. G., Beach, R., and Young, B. (1987). Increasing voting behavior by

asking people if they expect to vote. *Journal of Applied Psychology,* 72: 315-18.

17. What is the active ingredient in lasting commitments?

32. This sales goal passage is discussed in: Cialdini, R. B. (2001). *Influence: Science and Practice* (4th ed.). Boston: Allyn & Bacon.

33. The active/passive commitment study can be found in: Cioffi, D., and Garner, R. (1996). On doing the decision: effects of active versus passive commitment and self-perception. *Personality and Social Psychology Bulletin,* 22:133-44.

18. How can you fight consistency with consistency?

34. The research examining how preference for consistency increases with age can be found in: Brown, S. L., Asher, T., and Cialdini, R. B. (2005). Evidence of a positive relationship between age and preference for consistency. *Journal of Research in Personality,* 39:517-33.

19. What persuasion tip can you borrow from Benjamin Franklin?

35. Ben Franklin's strategy is described extremely well in: Aronson, E., Wilson, T.D., and Akert, R. M. (2005). *Social Psychology* (5th ed.). Englewood Cliffs, NJ: Prentice Hall.

36. The Ben Franklin quotation can be found in: Franklin, B. (1900). *The Autobiography of Ben Franklin* (J. Bigelow, ed.). Philadelphia: Lippincott (originally published in 1868).

37. The study that tested the Benjamin Franklin effect can be found in: Jecker, J., and Landy, D. (1969). Liking a person as a function of doing him a favor. *Human Relations,* 22:371-78.

20. When can asking for a little go a long way?

38. The even-a-penny-will-help study can be found in: Cialdini, R. B., and Schroeder, D. A. (1976). Increasing compliance by legitimizing paltry contributions: when even a penny helps. *Journal of Personality and Social Psychology,* 34:599-604.

21. Start low or start high? Which will make people buy?

39. The eBay study can be found in: Ku, G., Galinsky, A. D., and Murnigham, J. K. (2006). Starting low but ending high: A reversal of the anchoring effect in auctions. *Journal of Personality and Social Psychology,* 90:975-86.

22. How can we show off what we know without being labeled a show-off?

40. The study on using others to establish our credentials can be found in: Pfeffer, J., Fong, C. T., Cialdini, R. B., and Portnoy, R. R. (2006). Overcoming the self-promotion dilemma: Interpersonal attraction and extra help as a consequence of who sings one's praises. *Personality and Social Psychology Bulletin,* 32:1362-74.

23. What's the hidden danger of being the brightest person in the room?

41. The groups versus individuals study can be found in: Laughlin, P.R., Bonner, B., and Minor, A. (2002). Groups perform better than the best individuals on letters-to-numbers problems. *Organizational Behavior and Human Decision Processes,* 88:605-20.

24. Who is the better persuader? Devil's advocate or true dissenter?

42. The source of the *Columbia* investigation transcript is: Langewiesche, W. (2003). Columbia's last flight. *The Atlantic Monthly,* 292, 58-87.

43. The devil's advocate versus true dissenter study can be found in: Nemeth, C., Brown, K., and Rogers, J. (2001). Devil's advocate versus authentic dissent: stimulating quantity and quality. *European Journal of Social Psychology,* 31:707-20.

44. The evidence that using a devil's advocate can strengthen majority members' confidence in their original position can be found in: Nemeth, C., Connell, J., Rogers, J., and Brown, K. (2001). Improving decision making by means of dissent. *Journal of Applied Social Psychology,* 31:48-58.

25. When can the right way be the wrong way?

45. The firefighters' training research can be found in: Joung, W., Hesketh, B., and Neal, A. (2006). Using "war stories" to train for adaptive performance: Is it better to learn from error or success? *Applied Psychology: An International Review,* 55, 282-302.

26. What's the best way to turn a weakness into a strength?

46. The research showing the benefits of displaying competitors' prices on a company's webpage can be found in: Trifts, V., and Häubl,

G. (2003). Information availability and consumer preference: Can online retailers benefit from providing access to competitor price information? *Journal of Consumer Psychology,* 13:149–59.

47. The study demonstrating the effects of admitting weaknesses in law can be found in: Williams, K. D., Bourgeois, M., and Croyle, R. T.(1993). The effects of stealing thunder in criminal and civil trails. *Law and Human Behavior,* 17:597–609.

27. Which faults unlock people's vaults?

48. The small but cozy study can be found in: Bohner, G., Einwiller, S., Erb. H-P., and Siebler, F. (2003). When small means comfortable: relations between product attributes in two-sided advertising. *Journal of Consumer Psychology,* 13:454–63.

49. Another informative study on this topic can be found in: Pechmann, C. (1992). Predicting when two-sided ads will be more effective than one-sided ads: The role of correlational and correspondent inferences. *Journal of Marketing Research,* 29:441–53.

28. When is it right to admit that you were wrong?

50. The research on admitting mistakes can be found in: Lee, F., Peterson, C., and Tiedens, L. A. (2004). Mea culpa: Predicting stock prices from organizational attributions. *Personality and Social Psychology Bulletin,* 30:1636–49.

29. How can similarities make a difference?

51. The name-similarity study can be found in: Garner, R. (2005). What's in a name? Persuasion perhaps. *Journal of Consumer Psychology,* 15:108–16.

30. When is your name your game?

52. The quotations from the American version of *The Office* are from the episode entitled "The Coup."

53. The research examining the effects of names on major life decisions, such as careers and locations, can be found in: Pelham, B. W., Mirenberg, M.C., and Jones, J.T. (2002). Why Susie sells seashells by the seashore: Implicit egotism and major life decisions. *Journal of Personality and Social Psychology,* 82:469–87.

54. The study showing that people are more likely to marry those with similar-sounding names can be found in: Jones, J. T., Pelham, B. W., Carvallo, M., and Mirenberg, M. C. (2004). How do I love thee? Let me

count the Js: Implicit egotism and interpersonal attraction. *Journal of Personality and Social Psychology,* 87:665–83.

55. The study examining the effects of people's names on consumer preferences can be found in: Brendl, M. C., Chattopadhyay, A., Pelham, B. W., and Carvallo, M. (2005). Name letter branding: Valence transfers when product specific needs are active. *Journal of Consumer Research,* 32:405–15.

31. What tips should we take from those who get them?

56. The tipping study can be found in: van Baaren, R. B., Holland, R. W., Steenaert, B., and van Knippenberg, A. (2003). Mimicry for money: behavioral consequences of imitation. *Journal of Experimental Social Psychology,* 39:393–98.

57. The first posture-mirroring study can be found in: Chartrand, T.K., and Bargh, J. A. (1999). The Chameleon effect: the perception-behavior link and social interaction. *Journal of Personality and Social Psychology,* 76:893–910.

58. The study examining the consequences of posture-mirroring in negotiations can be found in: Maddux, W. W., Mullen, E., and Galinsky, A. D. (2008). Chameleons bake bigger pies and take bigger pieces: Strategic behavioral mimicry facilitates negotiation outcomes. *Journal of Experimental Social Psychology,* 44:461–68.

32. What kind of smile can make the world smile back?

59. The smiling research can be found in: Grandey, A. A., Fisk, G. M., Mattila, A. S., Jansen, K. J., and Sideman, L. A. (2005). Is "service with a smile" enough? Authenticity of positive displays during service encounters. *Organizational Behavior and Human Decision Processes,* 96: 38–55.

33. When is a loser a winner?

60. The source of the Australian beef study is: Knishinsky, A. (1982). *The effects of scarcity of material and exclusivity of information on industrial buyer perceived risk in provoking a purchase decision.* Unpublished doctoral dissertation, Arizona State University, Tempe.

34. What can you gain from loss?

61. The quotation was taken from: Greenwald, J. (July 22, 1985). "Cola-Cola's Big Fizzle." *Time.* In addition, an excellent account of the New Coke debacle can be found in: Thomas, O. (1986). *The Real Coke, the Real Story.* New York: Random House. A different facet of it is also

discussed in: Gladwell, M. (2005). *Blink: The Power of Thinking Without Thinking.* New York: Little, Brown, and Co.

62. The original loss aversion work can be found in: Kahneman, D, and Tversky, A. (1979). Prospect theory: an analysis of decision under risk. *Econometrica,* 47:263–91. More on loss aversion and a host of other biases in judgment and decision-making can be found in Thaler, R. H., and Sunstein, C. R. (forthcoming). *Nudge: Improving Decisions About Health, Wealth, and Happiness.* New Haven, CT: Yale University Press; and Gilovich, T., and Belsky, G. (1999). *Why Smart People Make Big Money Mistakes—and How to Correct Them.* New York: Simon & Schuster.

63. The effects of loss aversion on stockholder behavior is discussed more in depth in: Shell, G. R. (1999). *Bargaining for Advantage.* New York: Penguin Books.

64. Research demonstrating loss aversion in management-oriented decisions can be found in: Shelley, M. K. (1994). Gain/loss asymmetry in risky intertemporal choice. *Organizational Behavior and Human Decision Processes,* 59:124–59.

35. Which single word will strengthen your persuasion attempts?

65. The Xerox studies can be found in: Langer, E., Blank, A., and Chanowitz, B. (1978). The mindlessness of ostensibly thoughtful action: The role of "placebic" information in interpersonal interaction. *Journal of Personality and Social Psychology,* 36:639–42.

66. The studies showing the power of generating reasons in favor of a position can be found in: Maio, G. R., Olson, J. M., Allen, L., and Bernard, M. M. (2001). Addressing discrepancies between values and behavior: The motivating effect of reasons. *Journal of Experimental Social Psychology,* 37:104–17.

36. When might asking for all the reasons be a mistake?

67. The BMW versus Mercedes study can be found in: Wänke, M., Bohner, G., and Jurkowitsch, A. (1997). There are many reasons to drive a BMW: Does imagined ease of argument generation influence attitudes? *Journal of Consumer Research,* 24:170–77.

68. Two studies that support our advice on imagery are: Gregory, L. W., Cialdini, R. B., and Carpentar, K. M. (1982). Self-relevant scenarios as mediators of likelihood estimates and compliance: does imagining make it so? *Journal of Personality and Social Psychology,* 43:89–99; and Petrova, P. K., and Cialdini, R. B. (2005). Fluency of consumption imagery and the backfire effects of imagery appeals. *Journal of Consumer Research,* 32:442–52.

37. How can the simplicity of a name make it appear more valuable?

69. The stock-naming studies can be found in: Alter, A. L., and Oppenheimer, D. M. (2006). Predicting short-term stock fluctuations by using processing fluency. *Proceedings of the National Academy of Sciences,* 103:9369–72.

70. The source of the jargon-filled quotation is: Moore, B. (2006, October 9). The towers of babble: The worst excesses of workplace jargon can leave one begging for a translator—and a return to plain English. Retrieved from www.nypost.com/seven/10092006/atwork/the_ towers_of_babble_atwork_brian_moore.htm.

71. The study on the effects of using big words can be found in: Oppenheimer, D. M. (2006). Consequences of erudite vernacular utilized irrespective of necessity: Problems with using long words needlessly. *Applied Cognitive Psychology,* 20:139–56.

38. How can rhyme make your influence climb?

72. The rhyming research can be found in: McGlone, M. S., and Tofighbakhsh, J. (2000). Birds of a feather flock conjointly (?): rhyme as reason in aphorisms. *Psychological Science,* 11:424–28.

39. What can batting practice tell us about persuasion?

73. The contrast research can be found in: Tormala, Z. L., and Petty, R. E. (2007). Contextual contrast and perceived knowledge: Exploring the implications for persuasion. *Journal of Experimental Social Psychology,* 43:17–30.

40. How can you get a head start in the quest for loyalty?

74. The car wash study can be found in: Nunes J. C., and Dreze, X. (2006). The endowed progress effect: How artificial advancement increases effort. *Journal of Consumer Research,* 32:504–12.

41. What can a box of crayons teach us about persuasion?

75. The color name research can be found in: Miller, E. G., and Kahn, B. E. (2005). Shades of meaning: the effect of color and flavor names on consumer choice. *Journal of Consumer Research,* 32:86–92.

Notes

42. How can you package your message to ensure it keeps going, and going, and going?

76. One important source of information on consumers' confusion of Energizer and Duracell is: Lipman, Joanne (1990). "Too Many Think the Bunny Is Duracell's, Not Eveready's." *The Wall Street Journal* (July 31), B1.

77. An excellent review of the research in the role of memory in advertising can be found in: Keller, K. L. (1991). Memory factors in advertising: The effect of retrieval cues on brand evaluations. In A. A. Mitchell (ed.), *Advertising Exposure, Memory, and Choice* (11–48). Mahwah, NJ: Erlbaum. A more general review of the research on memory aids can be found in: Tulving, E., and Thompson, D. M. (1973). Encoding specificity and retrieval processes in episodic memory. *Psychological Review*, 80:352–73.

78. We have previously articulated our recommendations for public health campaigns in: Goldstein, N. J., and Cialdini, R. B. (2007). Using social norms as a lever of social influence. In A. Pratkanis (ed.), *The Science of Social Influence: Advances and Future Progress*. Philadelphia, PA: Psychology Press. The book is an excellent academic resource covering recent social influence research.

79. One study showing that alcohol can make persuasive messages more effective can be found in: MacDonald, T., Fong, G., Zanna, M., and Matrineau, A. (2000). Alcohol myopia and condom use: Can alcohol intoxication be associated with more prudent behavior? *Journal of Personality and Social Psychology*, 78:605–19.

43. What object can persuade people to reflect on their values?

80. The Halloween study examining the effect of a mirror can be found in: Beaman, A. L., Klentz, B., Diener, E., and Svanum, S. (1979). Self-awareness and transgression in children: Two field studies. *Journal of Personality and Social Psychology*, 37:1835–46.

81. The littering research can be found in: Kallgren, C. A., Reno, R. R., and Cialdini, R. B. (2000). A focus theory of normative conduct: When norms do and do not affect behavior. *Personality and Social Psychology Bulletin*, 26:1002–12.

82. For more discussion on the problems with surveillance, see: Cialdini, R. B., Petrova, P. K., and Goldstein, N. J. (2004). The hidden costs of organizational dishonesty. *Sloan Management Review*, 45:67–73.

83. The research on having people state their names can be found in: Diener, E., Fraser, S. C., Beaman, A. L., and Kelem, R. T. (1976). Effects of deindividuation variables on stealing among Halloween trick-or-treaters. *Journal of Personality and Social Psychology*, 33:178–83.

84. The eyes research can be found in: Bateson, M., Nettle, D., and Roberts, G. (2006). Cues of being watched enhance cooperation in a real-world setting. *Biology Letters*, 2:412–14.

44. Does being sad make your negotiations bad?

85. The *Sex and the City* quotations are from the episode entitled "The Domino Effect."

86. The sadness research can be found in: Lerner, J. S., Small, D. A., and Loewenstein, G. (2004). Heart strings and purse strings: carryover effects of emotions on economic decisions. *Psychological Science,* 15:337–41.

87. The research on how emotions reduce people's ability to discriminate between the magnitudes of numbers can be found in: Hsee, C. K., and Rottenstreich, Y. (2004). Music, pandas, and muggers: On the affective psychology of value. *Journal of Experimental Psychology: General,* 133:23–30.

45. What can make people believe everything they read?

88. The quotation from the Chinese political prisoner can be found on page 23 in: Lifton, R. J. (1961). *Thought Reform and the Psychology of Totalism*. New York: Norton. We found this quotation in: Gilbert, D. T. (1991). How mental systems believe. *American Psychologist, American Psychologists,* 46:107–19.

89. The research showing that people are inclined to believe others' claims when they are low on cognitive resources can be found in: Gilbert, D. T., Krull, D. S., and Malone, P. S. (1990). Unbelieving the unbelievable: Some problems in the rejection of false information. *Journal of Personality and Social Psychology,* 59:601–13; and Gilbert, D. T., Tafarodi, R. W., and Malone, P. S. (1993). You can't not believe everything you read. *Journal of Personality and Social Psychology,* 65: 221–33. Our chapter title was inspired by the title of the latter paper. For those interested in learning more about Gilbert's fascinating ideas and research on the topic of people's lack of ability to predict what will make them happy, see: Gilbert, D. T. (2006). *Stumbling on Happiness*. New York: Knopf.

90. The research showing how disrupting people's ability to think can increase compliance can be found in: Davis B. P., and Knowles, E. S. (1999). A disrupt-then-reframe technique of social influence. *Journal of Personality and Social Psychology,* 76:192–99; and in: Knowles, E. S., and Linn, J. A. (2004). Approach-avoidance model of persuasion: alpha and omega strategies for change. In Knowles, E. S., and Linn, J. A., (eds.), *Resistance and Persuasion* (117–48). Mahwah, NJ: Erlbaum.

46. Are trimeth labs boosting your influence?

91. The caffeine research can be found in: Martin, P. Y., Laing, J., Martin, R., and Mitchell, M. (2005). Caffeine, cognition and persuasion: Evidence for caffeine increasing the systematic processing of persuasive messages. *Journal of Applied Social Psychology,* 35:160–82.

47. How can technology impede persuasive progress?

92. The source of the story and quotations about no email Fridays can be found in: Horng, Eric. (2007, March 10). No e-mail Fridays transforms office. Retrieved from http://abcnews.go.com/WNT/story?id=2939232&page=1.

93. The studies demonstrating our overconfidence in how well our e-communications are understood can be found in: Kruger, J., Epley, N., Parker, J., and Ng, Z. (2005). Egocentrism over e-mail: Can we communicate as well as we think? *Journal of Personality and Social Psychology,* 89:925–36.

94. The research examining the differences between online and face-to-face negotiation can be found in: Morris, M., Nadler, J., Kurtzberg, T., and Thompson, L. (2002). Schmooze or lose: Social friction and lubrication in e-mail negotiations. *Group Dynamics: Theory, Research, and Practice,* 6:89–100.

95. The study examining the solution to the online negotiation difficulties can be found in: Moore, D. A., Kurtzberg, T. R., Thompson, L., and Morris, M. (1999). Long and short routes to success in electronically mediated negotiations: Group affiliations and good vibrations. *Organizational Behavior and Human Decision Processes,* 77:22–43.

48. How do you get to yes in any language?

96. The studies showing how advertisement effectiveness differs across cultures can be found in: Han, S., and Shavitt, S. (1994). Persuasion and culture: advertising appeals in individualistic and collectivist societies. *Journal of Experimental Social Psychology,* 30:326–50.

49. How can you avoid driving your cross-cultural influence into the rough?

97. The Jack Nicklaus story, including quotations, can be found in: Ferguson, D. (2005, March 7). Grieving Nicklaus meets press. Retrieved from www.thegolfgazette.com/print.php?sid=2074.

98. The cross-cultural consistency research involving Americans and Asians can be found in: Petrova, P. K., Cialdini, R. B., and Sills, S. J.

(2007). Consistency-based compliance across cultures. *Journal of Experimental Social Psychology,* 43:104–11.

99. The cross-cultural consistency versus social proof research involving American and Polish participants can be found in: Cialdini, R. B., Wosinska, W., Barrett, D. W., Butner, J., and Gornik-Durose, M. (1999). Compliance with a request in two cultures: The differential influence of social proof and commitment/consistency on collectivists and individualists. *Personality and Social Psychology Bulletin,* 25:1242–53.

50. When does letting the call go to voicemail cause a hang-up in your influence?

100. The answering machine study can be found in: Miyamoto, Y., and Schwarz, N. (2006). When conveying a message may hurt the relationship: Cultural differences in the difficulty of using an answering machine. *Journal of Experimental Social Psychology,* 42:540–47.

101. The idea that people from collectivistic cultures tend to place a greater emphasis on the relational function of communication than do people from individualistic cultures is discussed more in depth in: Scollon, R., and Scollon, S. W. (1995). *Intercultural Communication: A Discourse Approach.* Cambridge, UK: Blackwell.

102. The research showing how Japanese listeners tend to provide more feedback can be found in: White, S. (1989). Backchannels across cultures: A study of Americans and Japanese. *Language in Society,* 18: 59–76.

Epilogue

103. Readers can learn more about the U.K. fuel shortage of 2000 at: http://news.bbc.co.uk/2/hi/in_depth/world/2000/world_fuel_crisis/ default.stm.

Acknowledgments

This book is essentially a collection of insights from the fascinating science of social influence. We are extremely thankful to a long list of scientists who conducted the research that we had the pleasure of reporting throughout this manuscript. Without their work, *Yes!* wouldn't be a book; it'd be a pamphlet.

In creating *Yes!*, we've been fortunate to have access to another collection of insights—those of our colleagues, partners, family members, and students. In particular, we would like to thank Matt Goldstein, Amy Krasner, Nick Schweitzer, Judy Shapiro, Sheldon Shapiro, Vladas Griskevicius, Chad Mortensen, Leah Combs, Jennifer Ottolino, Miguel Prietto, Stuart Shoen, and Chaundra Wong for reviewing and providing feedback on various chapters of the book in the early stages; we are also grateful to Eli Finkel for calling the story in the preface to our attention. Thanks also to Dan Norris, Nick Pope, Dil Sidhu, Brian Ahearn, Kathy Fragnoli, Christy Farnbauch, John Fisher, and Tim Batchelor for offering their own examples of how they used the science of persuasion to good effect. Many thanks are also due to Daniel Crewe, whose comments and critiques were very valuable to the development of this manuscript.

Acknowledgments

We would like to express our gratitude to Bruce Nichols, our editor at Free Press, for his enthusiasm for the book and for his insightful suggestions from cover to cover. The book benefited a great deal from his recommendations—particularly the Pun Eradication Program. We also had the pleasure of working with Emily Loose, who was enormously valuable in helping us put the right finishing touches on the book.

In addition, we highly value and appreciate the continuing working partnership with both Gary Colleran and Anne Buckingham from the Influence at Work U.K. office. We're also lucky enough to have Bobette Gordon, who made our lives so much easier at every turn, allowing us to concentrate on writing the book instead of worrying about the details surrounding it. Her hard work and dedication to the success of this project have been invaluable. And finally, we are truly grateful to Jenessa Shapiro, Bernie Goldstein, and Adelle Goldstein for their critical feedback on all aspects of the book, and even more important, for their unending support.

Index

Index

Index

Index

About the Authors

Dr. Noah J. Goldstein is a faculty member at the UCLA Anderson School of Management. His scholarly research and writing have been published in many of the premier psychology and business journals. He has been awarded research fellowships and grants from several U.S. government institutions, including the National Science Foundation and the National Institutes of Health. He has also consulted for a number of corporate and government organizations, including Accenture, the United States Census Bureau, and the United States Forest Service.

Steve J. Martin is the Director of Influence At Work (UK). He has a background in sales and marketing and has written many articles that have been featured in a variety of business publications and the national press. He is co-author of the book *Sold!* and speaks and conducts training at conferences all over the world. He also regularly presents on the subject of influence and persuasion at a number of business schools, including Cranfield University and the Cass London Business School.

Dr. Robert B. Cialdini is Regents' Professor of Psychology and Marketing at Arizona State University. He is the world's most quoted expert in the field of influence and persuasion and the author of the groundbreaking book *Influence: Science and Practice,* which has sold over one million copies. His research appears in a wide range of academic and business journals and has attracted the attention of business and governments alike. In 2003, he was awarded the Donald T. Campbell Award for his distinguished contribution to the field of social psychology.